JOURNEY FROM THE EDGE

From Weaponized Survival to Self-Reclamation

by

Dr. Stephen Thompson DC DACM FAIHM

Published by Rooted Reclaimers
an imprint of Exile Press

Early readers said kind things

We shared a near-final draft with clinicians, educators, and community facilitators across disciplines. Here's how the work landed for them:

> "This book doesn't just talk about healing — it drags you (lovingly) to the mirror and says, *'Let's get real.'* ... If you've ever felt that surviving wasn't the same as living, *Journey from the Edge* will meet you exactly where you are.
>
> It refuses to romanticize resilience. Dr. Thompson exposes how our 'strength' can become armor that isolates us, how success can mask pain, and how even kindness can be weaponized for survival. Yet beneath that honesty runs a current of hope."
> — **Dr. Kristy Arneson, DC, LMT**, Family Medicine & Integrative Care, **Journeys**

> "A deeply insightful and compassionate look at how trauma influences every part of our lives."
> — **Shawntia Chester**

"A book rarely combines the insight of a well-trained, trauma-informed provider... Dr. Thompson's willingness to share his vulnerability and expertise will help anyone affected by trauma... This book is fascinating and healing!"
— **Dr Christine Gresham DACM LAc,** Petersburg Acupuncture & Herbal Medicine

Personal opinions only. Educational, not medical advice. For diagnosis or treatment, consult a licensed clinician.

Journey from the Edge: From Weaponized Survival to Self-Reclamation
by Dr. Stephen Thompson

Library of Congress Control Number: 2026937501

ISBN: 978-1-966779-10-0 (Paperback)
ISBN: 978-1-966779-11-7 (eBook)
ISBN: 978-1-966779-12-4 (Audiobook)

First Edition

Edited by Peter Liptak
Cover & Interior design by Peter Liptak

1. SELF-HELP / Post-Traumatic Stress Disorder (PTSD)
2. PSYCHOLOGY / Psychopathology / Post-Traumatic Stress Disorder.

Ordering Information: Special discounts available on quantity purchases by corporations, universities, and associations for sales promotions, premiums, fundraising, gifts and educational use. For details, contact info@rootedreclaimers.com.

Disclaimer: This book is designed to provide information, shared experiences, and motivation. It is sold with the understanding that the author and publisher are not engaged in rendering psychological, medical, or other professional services. If you are experiencing a mental health crisis or require expert assistance, please seek the services of a competent and licensed professional.

Publisher: Published by Rooted Reclaimers An imprint of Exile Press 729 N Washington Ave 6th Fl Minneapolis, MN 55401 rootedreclaimers.com

Dedication

For the breath that steadies you,
the movement that carries you,
the nourishment that sustains you,
and the connections that call you home.

To those who were never given a map yet found their way through, you are the reason *Journey from the Edge* exists.
You are the proof that even on the edge, life waits to be reclaimed.

About the Author

I'm Dr. Stephen Thompson, DC, DACM, FAIHM. I'm an integrative trauma specialist, educator, and fellow survivor who knows intimately what it costs to perform a strength you don't feel.

For over two decades, I've worked at the intersection of physiology, somatic practice, and system-aware care. My training spans chiropractic medicine, acupuncture, and integrative and functional approaches to chronic stress and inflammatory disease. But my deepest education came from living inside a nervous system shaped by pressure, vigilance, and expectation.

I founded Rooted Reclaimers to bridge a gap I kept seeing in both clinics and communities. We talk about mindset. We talk about resilience. But we rarely talk about Safety Budget. We rarely ask how much load a body is carrying, or how racism, classism, chronic threat, and systemic stress shape that load.

Context sets the load.

When the load is chronic, the nervous system adapts. Those adaptations are not flaws. They are intelligent survival responses.

The Four Pillars framework I developed, Breathe, Move, Nourish, Connect, was never meant to fix broken people. It was built to offer small, 60-second micro-moves that help exhausted survivors widen their window of tolerance without overwhelming their system. Body first. Capacity before performance.

I have taught in clinics, classrooms, and community spaces, supporting thousands of high-functioners, caregivers, organizers, and leaders who are tired of weaponized survival. My work translates complex neuroscience into practices that real nervous systems can actually use.

I wrote *Journey from the Edge* because I believe healing is not a private act of perfection. It is a shared practice of mending our fractures with gold. It is learning how to renegotiate survival plasticity into something softer, steadier, and more whole.

Reclamation is sacred work.

And we do it together.

Lets keep it honest before we move ahead

I've been grinding and building accolades since I was young. I bring this up to tell you that I know the pain of survival intimately. I'm someone who has messed-up, pushed way too hard, and I tried to outrun and outwork feelings that I needed to confront for a long time. If you have felt something similar, welcome. You're in the right place.

If you:

- Pretend to be ok when you are clearly not
- Keep chasing higher goals trying to fill a void of self-esteem
- Refuse to ask for help, even though you are drowning
- Feel guilty when you take an hour to yourself to rest

Exercise (one tiny experiment):

One hand on heart, one hand on belly (in any position), say to yourself or think: "I am worthy of love and respect," Or "I trust in my abilities and to make good decisions."=

A Note on Safety and Pace

THIS BOOK INVITES YOU into sensitive territory. Please go at a pace that feels right for your body today. You never need to push through discomfort to "do it right." If something feels too much, pause, skip ahead, or close the book. You can return later.

For immediate grounding, try the 60-second Grounding in chapter 6 or visit **rootedreclaimers.com/resources**. If you are in crisis or worried about your safety, contact your local emergency number or, in the U.S., call or text **988** for the Suicide & Crisis Lifeline.

Permission Slip: You Can Stop

This is a tangible reminder for self-pacing and stopping before any self-regulation or therapeutic practice, explicitly granting permission to lower threat response and enhance learning.

“I can stop at any time.”

“Less is allowed.”

“If my body says no, that’s ok too”

“Remember its just data, not failure.”

Why It Helps Consent lowers threat and increases real learning.

Important Reminders

Educational, not medical advice.

Pause check: breath, shoulders, jaw. You choose the pace.

One Lens, Many Lives

This book centers around Black and African-diasporic experiences because they reveal how bodies adapt under chronic threat, and how when given safety those same bodies not only live but learn to thrive. The patterns we explore show how weaponized survival, survival plasticity, and the long tail of stress show up across most communities: Indigenous, immigrant, working-class and rural white, Asian, Latinx, LGBTQ+, disabled, formerly incarcerated, and more. Your story belongs here. *I center one lens to illuminate many.*

You do not need to read this book straight through. Some chapters are explanatory. Others are experiential. The bolded terms link to the glossary for reference, not mastery. The practices are invitations, not assignments. If something feels like too much, skip it. *Orientation matters more than completion.*

ROOTED RECLAIMERS

FROM WEAPONIZED SURVIVAL TO SELF-RECLAMATION

Your Free Companion Practice Series

THE 7-DAY SAFETY BUDGET *RESET*

Move from Reading to Doing in Small, Body-First Steps

- 60-Second Safety Budget Check-in
- 4 Short Video Lessons (Under 10 Minutes)
- Printable Micro-Moves Starter Kit
- Audio Breath Practices + Guides
- Your On-Ramp to Community

→ Get Instant Access: ←

ROOTEDRECLAIMERS.COM/START

✓ Immediate Access

✓ Name + Email Only

Your first small step toward lasting change starts here.

Rooted Reclaimers

BODY-FIRST • EQUITY-CENTERED • COMMUNITY-HELD

Contents

Introduction

A Map Drawn in Scars

THIS BOOK WAS BORN from survival, reflection, and reaching for deeper healing. Not the kind sold in platitudes or quick fixes. The kind that demands you reorder the self you built just to survive. This work is for anyone who used mastery, humor, excellence, or stoic disposition as armor. For those who survived the worst the world could throw, then got asked to thrive without ever being taught how to heal after battle.

For the ones who looked around and saw the game was rigged. Survival was a triumph, yes. But it costs authenticity, intimacy, and creativity. Sometimes even joy. For those who built walls around their hearts and called it strength. Because in this world, vulnerability felt too dangerous to risk.

Journey from the Edge is for those who've survived more than they should have. I'm not a clinical psychologist, though I majored in clinical psychology in college and was mentored by a PhD Psychologist in graduate school. What's written here doesn't replace therapy or professional guidance. I wrote this from lived experience as a Black man, clinician, and survivor. But it's not just my story. It's a call to anyone carrying trauma in their body and their nervous system. Whether it came from personal harm, systemic injustice, or inherited hopelessness.

This book is not just the story of how my body learned to survive. It is a map for how bodies learn safety again. What I share here is personal, but it is not private. The patterns I describe live in nervous systems shaped by stress, threat, marginalization, and chronic demand. The tools that helped me heal are not mystical or exclusive. They are grounded in physiology, neuroscience, movement, nutrition, and relational repair. My story is the doorway. The work is meant to be shared.

This book is for people who've learned to armor up just to get through the day, and who are starting to wonder what it might mean to live and thrive, not just survive. I'm speaking to survivors, yes, but also to the clinicians, the curious minds, the healers, and the ones rebuilding their sense of self, piece by piece. I hope this book helps people name what they've carried, understand how their bodies adapted, and remember that reclamation is important, attainable work.

This book is also a reckoning with the structures that shaped our wounds: caste systems, economic hierarchies, racial violence, and systemic deprivation of food, housing, healthcare, and love. Trauma isn't just individual misfortune. It's cultural, systemic, and generational. Trauma isn't random. It's patterned. If it's patterned, it can be studied. If it can be studied, it can be interrupted. For ourselves and for those who come after.

I want to be clear. The theories posed in this and subsequent chapters are not completely settled scientific fact. These are novel and urgent clinical hypotheses, ones that trauma-informed medicine would do well to investigate more rigorously. The correlation between unresolved trauma and the epidemic rise of chronic inflammatory diseases is too profound to ignore, even when the cause is complex and multifactorial. There is a growing body of research exploring trauma theory, and it's my hope this body of work furthers the conversation.

So, what you'll find here is more than theory. It's lived experience braided with historical reality, cultural truth, neuroscience, and commitment to human dignity. It's the product of walking the long journey back to myself, though bruised, bloodied, and sometimes lost, but still lighting a lantern for anyone searching for their own way home.

There's a cost to survival nobody talks about. We celebrate those who "made it out" without accounting for the fractures left behind. We honor visible victories – degrees, promotions, accolades – without seeing the invisible sacrifices. We mistake resilience for wholeness. Brilliance for healing.

But, resilience isn't wholeness. Success isn't safety. Visibility isn't belonging.

My first understanding of these fractures didn't come from personal injury. It came from witnessing someone else's destruction.

I was a boy when I first saw Emmett Till's face in an old *Jet* magazine my parents kept. A mutilated Black body, brutalized past recognition, stared back across decades. Daring me to look away. I couldn't. I wouldn't. It was a modern-day lynching, not unlike what the country would witness generations later with George Floyd's murder by a Minneapolis police officer.

Until that moment, the civil rights stories told in my home felt important but distant. History. Something completed, and stored away. Honored but contained. Emmett's body broke that container. It pulled history out of safe storytelling and injected it straight into my bloodstream.

It wasn't history anymore. It was prophecy – a mirror and a warning.

There's an ancient wound stitched into Black existence in America. Seeing Emmett Till taught me what no classroom dared say. Black bodies were, and sometimes still are, permissible casualties in a system built for white Christian male dominance. Our existence itself was framed as provocation.

I was no longer a passive observer. I'd been conscripted into a rigged game. My body rendered suspicious by simply existing.

That moment shattered my assumptions about safety, belonging, and fairness itself. It altered the calculus of my daily existence. It reframed my people-pleasing tendencies not as personal quirks but as strategic survival mechanisms – tools to be unthreatening, to be impeccable, to offer no justification for violence or exclusion.

I learned early what many of my White classmates would never comprehend, the silent math running in the background of my mind: the constant modulation of voice, posture, vocabulary, and gaze. This is called *code-switching.* Code-switching is the practice of changing language, tone, posture, or behavior to appear acceptable in dominant spaces. It is not at all about deception, but survival. Over time, the nervous system learns that safety depends on constant self-monitoring, which is exhausting and costly. All to minimize triggering their unconscious biases. The emotional burden of simply existing while Black, the burden and exhaustion of being preemptively suspect. Of how others perceive your existence, while trying to remain calm and centered. These are the most exhausting inheritances of Blackness in America.

I started hunting for the missing pieces of our American story. School textbooks offered sanitized narratives of progress, triumph, and equality achieved. But I knew better. I sought out the unvarnished truth in the libraries, in elders' whispered wisdom, in documentaries and histories that dared to lift the veil. In our literary luminaries like Woodson, Baldwin, Hughes, Wright, and so many others. I learned that it was not about individual acts of racism. It was architecture. It was systems engineered for containment and erasure.

Housing policies penned Black families into ghettos. Educational policies starved Black schools of resources. Employment practices devalued Black labor. Healthcare systems treated Black bodies as disposable. None of this was by accident. This was coordinated, deliberate societal design. All of it devastating whole communities' futures.

Understanding this didn't make me cynical. It made me a realist. Wary of any narrative suggesting healing could happen without reckoning with the landscape that injured us.

Trauma isn't an isolated event. It's an ecosystem. If trauma is patterned, if injustice is structural, then our adaptations to survive it like hypervigilance, emotional numbing, people-pleasing, perfectionism, are not personal failings. They are ingenious strategies. They are the brain and body doing what they must to endure conditions hostile to human dignity.

When I say "patterns," I mean the repetitive decisions that we make individually

In our relationships, in our families, and in our communities, patterns are what trap us, but also what sets us free. When we shift our focus from destructive patterns to healthy patterns, we change. Building healthy patterns takes time, but by doing one small thing, over and over again, the body starts to accept it.

If you:

• Keep making the same decision that keeps you from your goals

• Fight, flight, freeze, or fawn before giving yourself a moment to think

• Get angry with yourself when you know you should do better and still don't

Try this Exercise: (one tiny experiment)

Be a bit more reflective this week. Pick one pattern you notice. Write on a piece of paper: "My pattern is _________". Then on the next line below it add: "It helped me survive once"

At the core of all survival is the nervous system's ability to change itself, and what science calls neuroplasticity. At its most basic, it means that neurons, our brain's messengers, can form new pathways when exposed to new conditions. But when trauma is the teacher, the brain learns fear. When betrayal is constant, it rewires for suspicion. When neglect is the baseline, it dulls sensitivity to preserve function.

What I later understood is that not all neuroplasticity is created equal. **Survival plasticity** is the ability to reshape one's behavior, perception, and internal rhythms under pressure, in hostile environments where safety is inconsistent or absent. The body and brain adapt to chronic stress by rewiring for speed, vigilance, efficiency, and control. In contrast, **privilege plasticity** grows in resourced environments – where experimentation is safe, failure is recoverable, and identity exploration does not come with life-altering consequences.

For trauma survivors, this means our brains, and consequently our bodies, are often shaped by threats, grief, shame, abandonment, and invisibility. The changes aren't theoretical – they're structural. The trauma gets stored not as memory, but as sensation, as chronic tension, and as inflammation. We stuff what we can't process into what I call the **closet**: an internal holding chamber where pain – loss, betrayal, and subversion – gets stored to keep us functional. Over time, once full, that closet leaks. And when it does, the consequences are not just emotional. They are physical.

If brain and body can be shaped by pain, they can be reshaped by safety, nourishment, and connection. Rewiring is possible. But it requires intention, time, and practice. Reconnecting to the body as both witness and participant in healing – through *breath*, *movement*, *nutrition*, and *connection*. This is why Rooted Reclaimers was created. It began as a question: what would healing look like if it were body-first, community-held, and paced for real nervous systems? What follows in this book became the foundation.

The psychic harm from systemic unfairness doesn't appear all at once. It accumulates slowly, discretely, across years. Across generations. It doesn't always explode into crisis. More often, it settles into exhaustion, detachment, or muted hopelessness. Easy to miss. Hard to name. This slow burn wears down the **trauma buffer** – the internal capacity we each have to manage adversity – until even ordinary stressors start to feel unbearable. Over time, that corrosion reaches deeper. It hollows out belief in progress, dulls ambition, and dims faith. When this kind of unseen injury is carried not by one person but by an entire community, the chances of trauma being passed down grow exponentially. It weaves into parenting, relationships, religion, education, politics. Even into the nervous systems of those not yet born.

The **emotional currency** we spend to achieve "normalcy" in hostile environments is astronomically higher than what's demanded of our privileged peers. Every promotion, every accolade, every success costs an unseen toll. Vigilance. Exhaustion. Often, profound loneliness.

Survival demands we become connoisseurs of injustice, reading every subtle cue for danger while pretending not to notice. A tightrope that frays a little more each year.

Even today, echoes of that first unfairness resurface when progress gets rolled back under the guise of protecting "traditional values"—values that too often mean protecting mediocrity cloaked in Whiteness while punishing excellence when it wears Black or brown skin.

James Baldwin shared cogent insights on racism during a taping of the Dick Cavett show in the '60's. He said, "Once you turn your back on this society, you may die. Not from paranoia, but from real danger. Visible in the face of every cop, every boss, every gatekeeper."

This is the reality into which we are born, into which we must build our lives. It shapes where we live, where we work, how much of ourselves we reveal, and who we dare to trust.

And yet. This isn't the whole story. Because even amid this landscape, healing is possible. The kind that requires everything: your grace, your courage, your grief, your tenderness, your persistence, and your forgiveness.

Healing demands we face the adaptations we once called strengths and recognize the wounds that forged them. It asks us to grieve the years lost to fear. The opportunities missed because hypervigilance hijacked joy. The love we couldn't fully receive because we were too busy scanning for danger.

There will be moments on this journey when you want to turn back. When the mask feels safer than raw truth. When the numbness of survival beckons like an old friend.

But please, STAY.

Stay, because like Kintsugi reveals gold within the fractures of broken pottery, our experiences of trauma, when acknowledged and integrated, can transform perceived weaknesses into visible sources of strength and wisdom.

Because, you are not your trauma. You are not the story your pain tried to tell about you. You are not the mask you had to wear to survive.

In fact, you are living proof that healing is possible.

This is not a blueprint for perfection. It's a map drawn in scars and dreams. It's an invitation to persistence, to tenderness, and to the reclamation of the original self that trauma tried to bury.

Welcome to the journey back to you.

You do not have to walk it alone anymore.

Preface

The Slap Heard Around the World

On March 27, 2022, during the live broadcast of the 94th Academy Awards, the world watched a moment of raw, unscripted emotion unravel onstage. Will Smith, one of the highest-paid and most beloved actors of our time, rose from his seat, walked calmly to center stage, and slapped comedian Chris Rock in the face. It was in response to a joke Rock made about Jada Pinkett Smith, Will's wife, a woman whose public journey with alopecia had already made her a target of speculation and ridicule.

The collective gasp wasn't just about the physicality of it. It was about who did it. This wasn't a volatile celebrity or a desperate actor looking for attention. This was Will Smith, a man who had spent decades mastering the art of charisma, crafting a public image of control, kindness, and good-natured resilience. In a single moment, that image cracked, and what spilled out was decades in the making.

In his memoir, *Will*, Smith speaks openly about his childhood, about growing up with an abusive father and the deep guilt he carried for not stepping in to protect his mother. He calls himself a coward for freezing in those formative moments. That guilt metastasized into a lifelong vow to always protect, always fix, always be the hero. But what happens when that hero is triggered, when protection becomes performance, and the script falls away?

This is what trauma does. It doesn't disappear because you're rich. It doesn't dissolve in fame. It waits. It shapes you quietly, programming your body and mind to respond with ancient, survival-driven patterns. And when the right button gets pushed, even in front of millions of people, the past can break through the present like a wave crashing over a weathered dam.

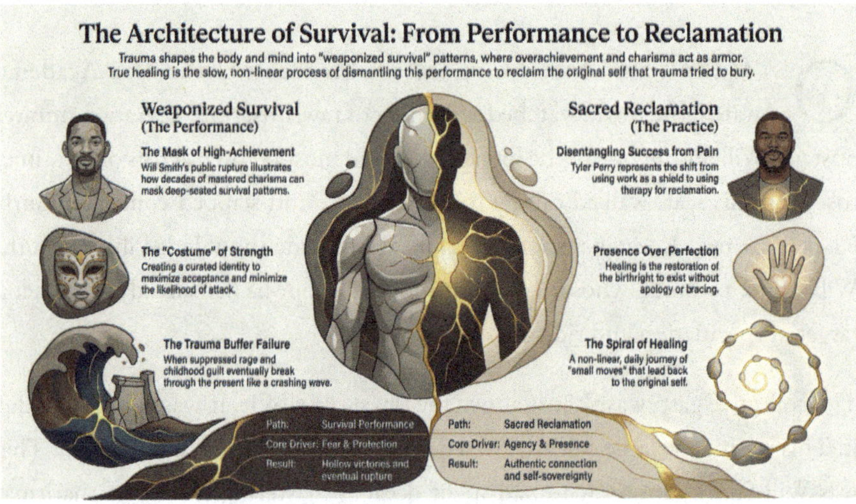

But not every story ends in rupture. Tyler Perry offers a parallel tale. Like Smith, Perry experienced extreme abuse in childhood. His father beat him. He was sexually abused by multiple adults. And like many trauma survivors, he built an empire from the ashes, using work, faith, and creativity as a shield. But unlike many, Perry sought intensive therapy later in life. He began the hard work of disentangling his success from his pain. In 2023, he spoke publicly about how therapy helped him reclaim parts of himself he didn't know were still buried under the trauma.

Both men are testaments to the truth this book is grounded in: You can be famous and broken. You can be beloved and unwell. You can be powerful and still be at the mercy of wounds that haven't healed. And the work of healing isn't glamorous, it's daily, humbling, and often invisible. But it's the only road to true reclamation.

This book is not about judging that slap. It's about understanding what makes it possible. What happens to the inner child when his needs are ignored for decades? What happens when armor becomes identity, and rage becomes the only language left that feels honest?

Journey from the Edge begins here, with the acknowledgment that none of us are immune to our past. And all of us, no matter how successful, still deserve space to come home to ourselves.

PART I

Weaponized Survival

When adaptation becomes armor.

Chapter 1

The Cost of the Costume

SURVIVAL DEMANDS ENDURANCE. THEN it demands performance, creativity, and cunning. Not simply wearing a mask to fool others. It's the engineering of an entire identity. The mannerisms, affect, posture, voice modulation, ambition calibration, all stitched together to maximize the probability of acceptance and minimize the likelihood of an attack.

For many trauma survivors, staying alive, safe, and maintaining connection required becoming what others needed, expected, or tolerated. The authentic self, with its full emotional range, its vulnerabilities, its unvarnished truths, was often too dangerous to present openly. A costume was created. A curated self, stitched together from necessity, fear, and the instinct to belong in a world that punished authenticity.

Roles That Keep Us Chosen (and Tired)

The costume varies. For some, it's the overachiever, masking insecurity with accolades. For others, the caregiver, disappearing into the needs of others to avoid abandonment. For some, the rebel, using defiance as a shield against betrayal and wit to skewer aggressors. For others, the invisible one, fading into the background to minimize risk.

Each version served a purpose. Each version was intelligent in its origin. The costume wasn't a mistake or a weakness. It was a highly sophisticated adaptation to unsafe environments, designed to maximize survival by minimizing exposure.

The tragedy isn't that the costume exists. The tragedy is how completely it can fuse with identity over time, until the wearer forgets it was ever a separate construction.

As a child navigating a volatile world, I learned quickly that roles were currency. Every costume I wore bought me safety, approval, or distance from harm. At first, these adaptations were brilliant. They kept me fed, praised, and protected. Over time, they became mandatory. What once helped me survive slowly taught my nervous system that rest was dangerous and authenticity was a liability.

At first, the costume is a tool designed to create and maintain safety in environments that challenge that notion. Consciously worn, adjusted, removed depending on the situation. But when unsafe environments are constant, the costume hardens. It ceases to be something worn for protection and becomes something inhabited. The survival-adapted self becomes the only self the outside world is allowed to see.

The problem is the survival costume is often reinforced by external rewards. The world applauds the high achiever, the loyal caregiver, the charming rebel. Recognition and approval create powerful feedback loops, making it even harder to recognize that the version of self being celebrated is not the whole story. Many survivors internalize this approval as conditional. As long as they perform the expected role, they are acceptable. If they falter, reveal weakness, or show unmet needs, they risk rejection or abandonment. This reinforcement deepens identification with the costume, making the thought of removing it feel life-threatening. Without the costume, who are you? Without the armor, how will you survive the storms sure to come?

If you are known as "the good one," this is for you

Have you noticed that people love you most when you are helpful to them or high performing, or calming in their presence? Yeah, it's a good feeling. The problem is that good feelings can also become a cage. Eventually, the body and mind get tired of needing to earn love.

If you:

- Say yes too quickly, then regret it minutes or hours later
- Feel so disconnected that you don't know what you need until you are already burned out
- Worry people won't like the "real" you

Exercise (One tiny experiment):
If someone asks a favor or request of you, before responding take a full 10 second breath, 4-5 second inhale and 4-5 second exhale. In your head or out loud say, "Let me check." That creates seeds of boundaries.

Try This Now: 60-Second Boundary Check

Learning to set boundaries is not about pushing people away. It's about giving your nervous system proof that you have a choice. A boundary is your body's way of saying, "This is where I end and you begin." For those of us trained in the art of the chameleon, this can feel terrifying, like a betrayal of the very role that kept us safe. We start small, with a single breath and a single phrase, reclaiming our space one moment at a time.

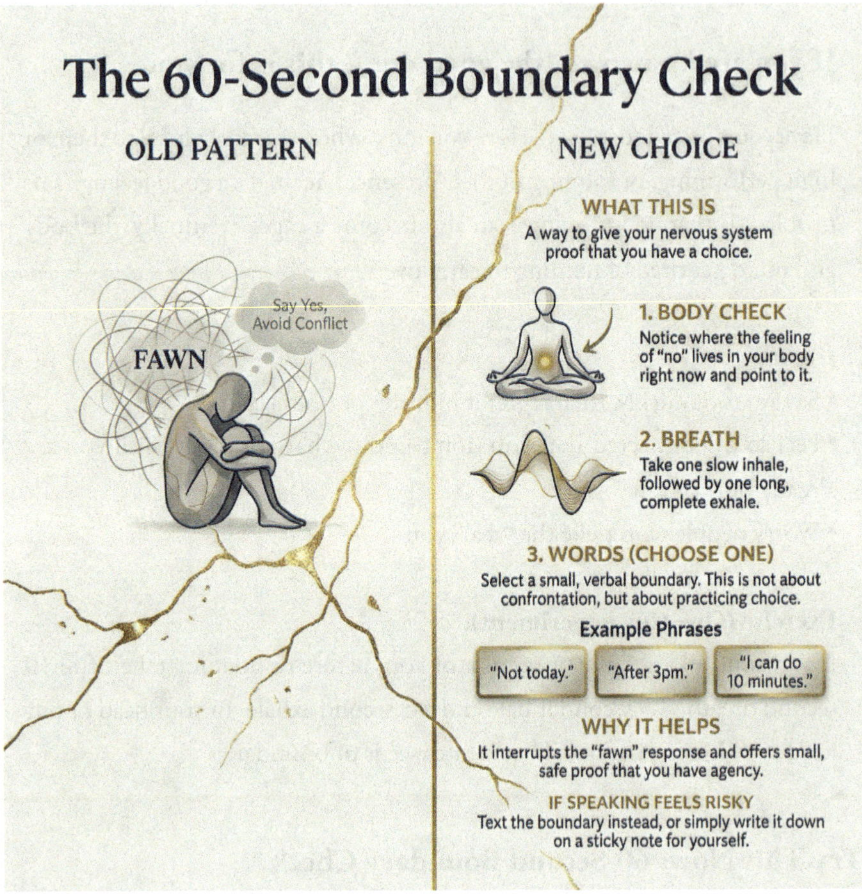

The Physiological Bill Comes Due

The cost of this survival strategy is immense. The deeper the investment in the costume, the more distant the relationship to the authentic self becomes. Emotional needs are dismissed or distorted. Vulnerability, once punished, is internally policed before anyone else has the chance to react. Joy and pleasure become performative. Anger becomes explosive or inaccessible. Grief turns into chronic numbness or crippling shame.

Physiologically, the dissonance exacts its own toll. Living in perpetual agitation and performance keeps the nervous system activated, even when no immediate threat is present. Hypervigilance becomes baseline programming. Over time, chronic activation reshapes emotional patterns, cognitive processes, and even physical health, setting the stage for anxiety, depression, autoimmune issues, relational dysfunction, and many of the lifestyle diseases, including heart disease, diabetes, and cancer we see at the community level.

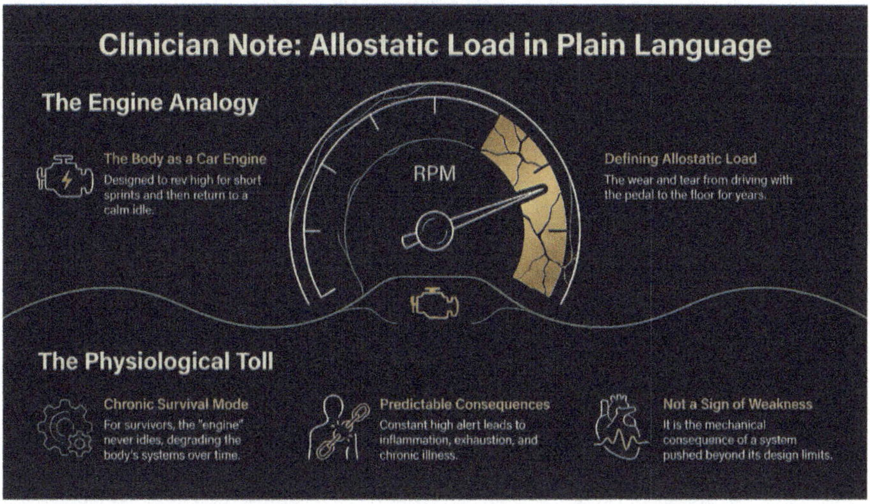

Clinician Note: Allostatic Load in Plain Language

Think of your body's stress response system like a car engine. It's designed to rev high for short sprints (like flooring it to merge onto a highway) and then return to a calm idle. **Allostatic load** is the wear and tear that happens to the engine when you're forced to drive with the pedal to the floor for hours, days, or years without a break.

For survivors in chronic survival mode, the "engine" never gets to idle. This constant state of high alert degrades the body's systems over time, leading to inflammation, exhaustion, and illness. It's not a sign of weakness; it's the predictable mechanical consequence of a system being pushed beyond its design limits for too long.

Healing requires confronting these questions honestly. It demands a reckoning with the reality that the survival costume, while once necessary, is no longer enough. It demands grieving the lost time, relationships, and pieces of selfhood sacrificed to survival performance. It demands acknowledging that safety bought at the price of self-erasure isn't safety at all.

The Cost of Being Good

Kindness, as an ideal, is often celebrated rhetorically but punished practically. In environments marked by systemic inequality, emotional dysregulation, or survival-driven social dynamics, to be truly kind, not performatively but constitutionally, exacts a heavy toll. That strategy carries a cost. Emotional currency.

I learned to trade parts of myself for safety. I learned that by preemptively fulfilling expectations, by diminishing my own needs and maximizing the comfort of others, I could minimize threats to my psychological and physical integrity. The cost was cumulative and invisible, the way a stress fracture develops in a bone long before it breaks. In the American social structure, a structure still fundamentally shaped by white patriarchal norms, empathy is often mistaken for weakness, and emotional range is frequently mischaracterized as instability. In that schema, the "good boy" becomes the soft target. Boundaries, when eventually asserted, are seen not as acts of self-preservation but as betrayals of the role others expect you to play.

When emotional currency depletes, the debt is paid by the body. Mental fog, irritability, escapism cravings, and physical symptoms surface when the trauma buffer reaches saturation. I liken this to a spaceship with plasma shields. Each microaggression, betrayal, or unmet need is a hit against the shields. Without rest and reinforcement, the shields eventually fail. When they do, real and sometimes catastrophic damage occurs.

Survival offers three primary options once shields fail. First, to build impossibly stronger shields – hyperindependence, hypervigilance, extreme emotional armor. Second, to evade incoming fire – stealth, diplomacy, avoidance, detachment. Third, and most dangerous, to counterattack with unregulated force. To destroy the perceived threat completely, even at the risk of self-destruction.

For many trauma survivors operating in survival plasticity, the third option is often unconscious and deeply suppressed until a final, desperate act. The abused partner who lashes out fatally. The codependent who engineers their own escape through cheating, addiction, betrayal. The professional who self-sabotages a career they can no longer sustain. These aren't random acts of dysfunction. They're survival strategies, activated too late.

Growing up as a Black kid in racially hostile America, I understood instinctively that even righteous anger could be lethal, not for others, but for me. My anger could be weaponized against me with terrifying speed by law enforcement, by teachers, or by simple misinterpretation of my body language. To survive, I learned to mask even justified rage. I reinforced my "good boy" costume with authenticity, not rage. Because survival demanded it.

Case Vignette: People-Pleasing in Practice

In early life, I became the kid who never missed school, who volunteered for clubs, who became the teacher's aide without fawning for favor. I positioned myself adjacent to power not to dominate but to shield myself. If the adults approved of me, perhaps the bullies would hesitate. If I was seen as "the good one," perhaps I could avoid closer scrutiny, deeper exposure. Kindness became strategic as well as moral.

Service and excellence were interwoven into my family legacy: doctors, lawyers, social workers, educators. Being of service was a collective calling. That calling, when coupled with trauma, created a feedback loop where goodness and kindness were both shield and shackle. To be good was to survive. To be good was to exhaust oneself trying to outpace systemic forces far larger than any individual could dismantle alone.

Even religion, while providing community and rituals of belonging, carried its own small-t traumas. Forced church attendance as an adolescent agnostic taught me the subtle violence of being "strongly urged" into performative belief, not by malice, but by fear and longing for connection. It was a microcosm of the larger social contract. Survive by adapting, by accommodating, by suppressing what cannot be safely expressed.

The mask of goodness is particularly insidious because it disguises hypervigilance as virtue. It masks the exhaustion of caring about everything under the guise of moral superiority. Yet it's easier, neurologically, psychologically, existentially, to care about nothing (apathy) than to sustain hypervigilance indefinitely. Every act of empathy costs energy. Every boundary suppressed costs energy. Every betrayal costs energy. Trauma survivors moving through a world ill-equipped to see the cost, continue to curate masks and costumes, not just faces, but entire embodied performances that allow us to survive spaces hostile to emotional range, systemic critique, and authentic selfhood.

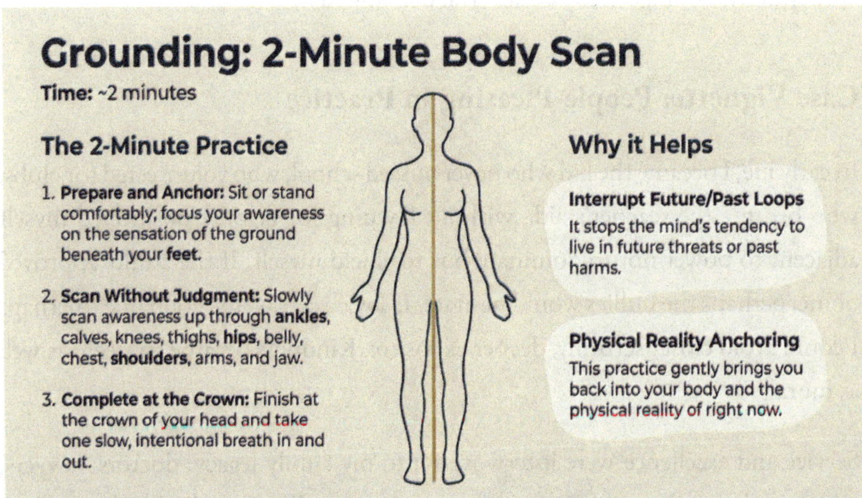

Why it helps: This practice gently brings you back into your body in the present moment. It interrupts the mind's tendency to live in future threats or past harms, and anchors you in the physical reality of *right now*.

The process of loosening the costume is slow. It begins not with grand declarations but with subtle acts of honesty. Noticing where you are performing and where you are present, where you are managing perception and where you are truly being seen. It requires reconnecting with the breath and creating spaces, internally and relationally, where the authentic self can emerge without immediate fear of punishment. There will be moments of profound discomfort. Parts of yourself long buried will surface, bringing grief, anger, and longing. Relationships built on the expectation of the costume may falter or end. New boundaries will need to be drawn. New vulnerabilities will need to be navigated.

This is the work. The journey home demands you honor the brilliance that built the costume but refuse to let it define you permanently. It demands you respect the intelligence that built the armor but commit to the slow labor of laying it down. You were never meant to be a permanent performance. You were meant to be alive. Survival required a mask. Healing demands your face.

Chapter 2

The Closet We Stuff Our Pain Into

SURVIVAL, FOR MOST OF us, didn't leave time for full processing. It demanded quick adaptations. Move on, stay strong, don't look back. When overwhelming experiences happened – direct abuse, big betrayals, sudden losses, humiliations, or small daily wounds that piled up like layers of dust – our bodies, minds, and spirits had to find a way to keep functioning. Phrases like "I'm fine" and "We don't need to talk about it" become wrapping paper for packaging and compartmentalizing our trauma.

Why? Because the body records every interaction with the external world.

Trauma, particularly when it's sustained and repetitive, does not simply dissipate once the acute threat has passed. It seeks containment – originally meant to be temporary – not just in some nebulous "psyche," but in the dense tangible tissues of the body itself: musculature, joints, fascia, and organ systems. To manage this, the human system developed a kind of internal storage mechanism. A mental, emotional, and physiological matrix I call the "closet" where unprocessed experiences could be tucked away for later. It's the place where unprocessed pain, unresolved betrayals, and unspoken griefs are hidden away when the conscious mind cannot afford to deal with them directly at the time of the offense.

Numb, Busy, or "Fine": Avoidance Strategies

The closet wasn't a flaw, and it wasn't abstract. It was a survival feature, and it was somatic and material. This closet gave us the ability to compartmentalize pain that would have otherwise immobilized us. It protected our ability to work, to parent, to show up in a world that demanded performance, not vulnerability. Without this mechanism, many of us wouldn't have made it through childhood, adolescence, or early adulthood intact–if at all.

Every survivor builds their closet differently. Some closets are reinforced with muscle – rigid posture, clenched jaws, compressed diaphragms. Some closets are built with dissociation – a numbness so pervasive that whole parts of the body might as well be foreign. Some closets are built with compulsion, workaholism, perfectionism, and addiction to achievement, sex, drugs, and other facades. All closets, however, share one devastating feature. They isolate the wounded parts of ourselves from both internal and external connection. What can't be named can't be grieved. What can't be grieved cannot be healed.

Symptoms That Are Really Signals

The closet lives in joints that ache without obvious cause, in the persistent inflammation that no diet or medication seems to tame, in the migraines, the irritable bowels, the unexplained fatigue. The body doesn't merely "store stress" as a convenient metaphor. It's possible that the "closet" may act as a kind of internal quarantine system, isolating emotional and energetic toxins that, if fully released into the system at once, would overwhelm the organism's ability to function.

Over time, this strategy of isolation may begin to backfire. This backfire can be a slow, physical leak, manifesting as inflammation, migraines, or autoimmune issues we've discussed.

But it can also be a sudden, catastrophic failure of the door itself. The moment when the closet is so full of unresolved trauma that one small, seemingly minor incident, a disagreement at work, a confrontation with a stranger, is all it takes to blow the hinges off. The resulting explosion of rage or grief can feel completely out of proportion to the event, leaving both the survivor and those around them stunned. This is not a sign of being "out of control." It's the predictable, physical outcome of a containment system pushed past its limits.

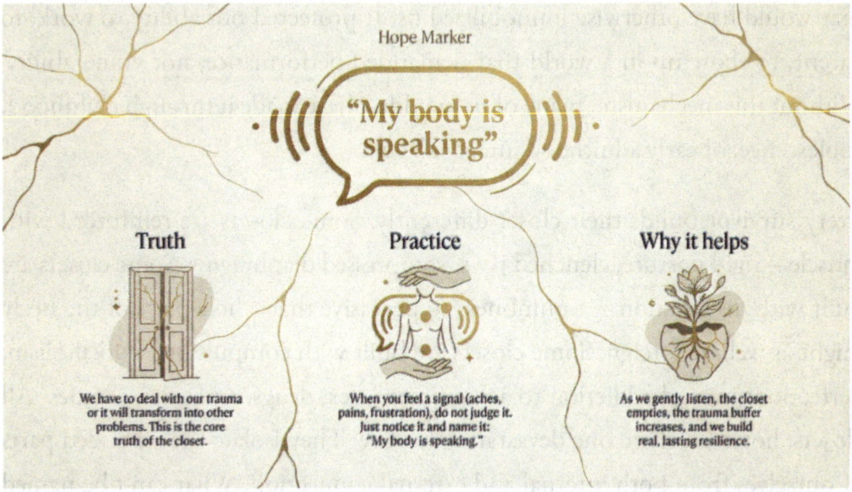

The immune system, confused by the presence of these walled-off toxins, may attack the body's own tissues in a desperate attempt to neutralize a threat it can't fully recognize and discern. The closet, then, isn't just a psychological metaphor for denial or suppression. It's, most likely, a somatic structure that has real physiological consequences over time. Fascia is the first place to investigate for this phenomenon.

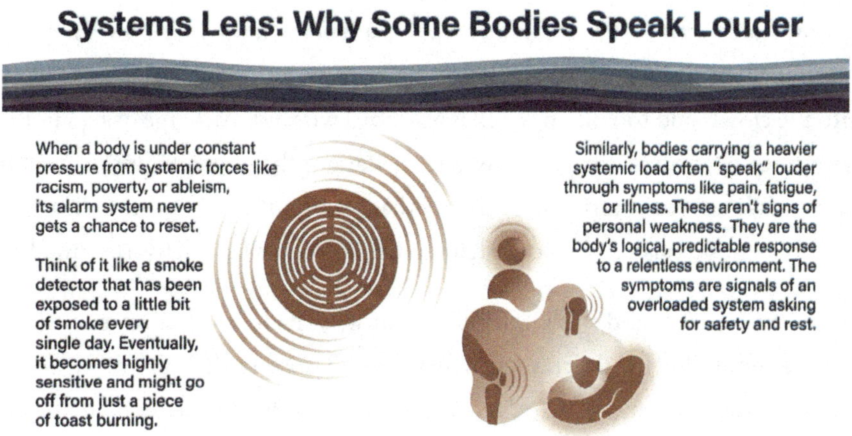

Systems Lens: Why Some Bodies Speak Louder

When a body is under constant pressure from systemic forces like racism, poverty, or ableism, its alarm system never gets a chance to reset. Think of it like a smoke detector that has been exposed to a little bit of smoke every single day. Eventually, it becomes highly sensitive and might go off from just a piece of toast burning.

Similarly, bodies carrying a heavier systemic load often "speak" louder through symptoms like pain, fatigue, or illness. These aren't signs of personal weakness. They are the body's logical, predictable response to a relentless environment. The symptoms are signals of an overloaded system asking for safety and rest.

Our bodies also come equipped with a natural buffer system, a biological resilience bank account that absorbs shocks. Minor "small t" traumas (a harsh word, a broken trust, a minor accident) and even manageable "Big T" traumas (grief, early loss, physical injury) can often be processed gradually without overwhelming the entire system. This is what we usually think of when we say someone is "resilient." The body, through its neural networks, endocrine system, and immune responses, can absorb and adapt to stress. Up to a point.

The trouble arises when that buffer system becomes saturated. There's a limit to how much cumulative trauma and stress anybody, no matter how strong or disciplined, can silently bear. When too many unresolved experiences are stuffed into the closet, and too much shock is absorbed without discharge or repair, the system begins to break down. Slowly at first—fatigue that doesn't improve, minor pains that linger, or emotional sensitivity that seems out of proportion. But over time, the signs escalate. What once felt manageable starts to feel insurmountable.

One way to understand this is to think about what happens after a car accident. Immediately following the crash, you may feel stiff, sore, rattled. The body, flooded with adrenaline and cortisol, races to stabilize itself. Within a few days, the pain may seem to resolve. You return to work, to life, grateful that things weren't worse. But if the trauma was not fully processed, if the physical damage wasn't rehabilitated properly, if the shock wasn't addressed, then the injury doesn't actually disappear. It simply gets locked away, deep in the musculoskeletal and fascial systems. Fast forward twenty years, and the same individual may develop arthritis, chronic neck pain, or unexplained migraines, often localized precisely where the body first absorbed the trauma. This isn't a coincidence. It's the closet at work.

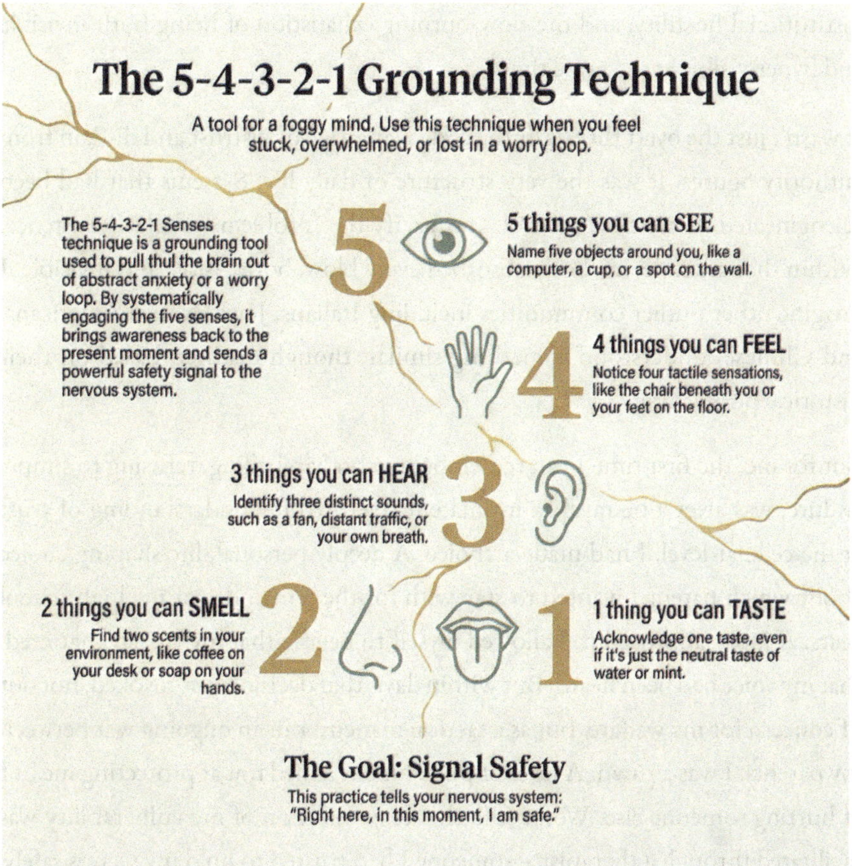

Why it helps: This exercise pulls your brain out of abstract anxiety and grounds it in the physical reality of your current environment. It sends a simple, powerful signal to your nervous system: "Right here, in this moment, I am safe."

Listening to the Body's Revolt

I don't remember exactly when my body first spoke to me in a language I could no longer ignore. It wasn't a singular moment of epiphany or collapse. It was a slow accumulation. A stacking of signals that grew louder over time until denial became impossible. Even though legally the apartheid state in America had "ended" with the civil rights victories of 1968, the lived experience remained something far different. A landscape marked by hundreds of microtraumas, constant institutional hostility, and the slow-burning exhaustion of being both invisible and hyper-visible at the same time.

It wasn't just the overt threats or the coded language of distrust and disdain from authority figures. It was the very structure of daily life. Systems that had been re-engineered to contain, control, and pacify the "problem" of Black existence. Within that crucible, my body absorbed every blow, both visible and invisible. I imagine other outlier communities including Italians, Jews, Native Americans, and Chinese, understood something similar, though distinct, based on their historical positioning.

But for me, the first time I can remember my body rebelling, refusing to simply endure, was after a betrayal so intimate it fractured my understanding of trust at the cellular level. I had made a choice. A deeply personal, life-shaping choice about which parent I wanted to stay with for the remainder of my high school years. A judge approved it. I allowed myself to believe that my agency mattered, that my voice had been heard. But within days, that decision was revoked, not out of concern for my welfare, but as a tactical maneuver in an ongoing war between my parents. I was a pawn. A lever of punishment aimed not at protecting me but at hurting someone else. Worse still, the weaponization of my vulnerability was facilitated through a therapist – someone I had trusted to hold my secrets safely. Words I had spoken in confidence were twisted and used against me. There is no betrayal quite so devastating as realizing that even your attempts to heal can be weaponized.

My body responded the only way it knew how. With rage transmuted into consumption. My drug of choice was food, specifically, pizza. Papa John's became my daily confession, my penance, my sedative. I was eating an entire large pizza almost every day, punishing myself for my perceived weakness, for my inability to resist the currents pulling me away from autonomy and into helplessness. Not gluttony. This was deep profound grief. This was my body attempting to create a barrier, a buffer, against a world that had proven itself indifferent at best and predatory at worst. This was my attempt to regain control over at least one arena of existence, what entered my body, until I could regain control over what entered my mind and heart.

Meanwhile, the parent tasked with protecting me was too deeply entangled in their own narrative of fear and victimhood to see the collateral damage being inflicted. Survival plasticity, that frantic, duct-tape adaptation to chaos, became my primary operating mode. It would guide me for the next year of my life, until community and movement intervened to begin the slow process of reclamation.

One of my closest friends unknowingly threw me a lifeline. He began running with me late at night. Not pushing, not lecturing, just running. Movement reconnected me to my body in ways that words never could. The repetitive thud of footfalls on pavement, the burning of lungs in cold air, and the ache and flex of my muscles under strain these sensations reminded me that I was alive. That I was still mine. More importantly, through that act of shared suffering, I rebuilt something even more critical: trust. Trust in another human being outside of myself. Trauma had taught me early that the safest hands were always my own. This friend helped me remember, or maybe taught me for the first time, that sometimes safety and healing can be shared, and that navigating trauma can be facilitated through somatic involvement.

The trauma adaptations did not vanish, of course. They simply evolved. The nice boy, the volunteer, the teacher's aide, the one always positioned near power but never so close as to be perceived as a threat. All these masks grew stronger, more polished. Adults adored me. Authority figures trusted me. Peers liked me. They heaped praise upon me daily, further reinforcing the survival mechanisms that shielded the deeper fractures inside. Fear of shame and exposure became the prime directive guiding every interaction of my mind, body, and spirit. Every adaptive move was designed to protect the wounded core from scrutiny, to preserve the carefully curated illusion of resilience and functionality.

The body did not stop speaking, of course. It adapted, compensated, and reconfigured itself around wounds both acknowledged and unacknowledged. If necessary, it will calcify those wounds into architecture—somewhat like a cancer. In this way, I was grooming myself for ultimate survival, not through brute strength, but through anticipatory adaptation, perpetual emotional reconnaissance, and mastery of every nuance of human expectation and disappointment. What my body understood was that in this world, survival is not guaranteed, and dignity is not given freely. It must be protected, curated, and sometimes fabricated until true healing becomes possible. And for those of us growing up under systems designed for our containment rather than our liberation, survival was an act of peaceful rebellion. Every day I endured was an act of protest. Every mask was a shield. Every smile was a weapon sharpened by necessity.

The cost of that survival would not fully reveal itself for years. But the first fissures, the first quiet cracks were already forming beneath the surface. Waiting for their own reckoning.

Chapter 3

When Survival Becomes a Masterpiece

THE WORLD TAUGHT YOU that staying alive required becoming someone else. So you did. You became exceptional at it. But no one told you that the same adaptations that saved you could eventually hollow you out. Survival isn't failure. It's brilliance carved from adversity, strategic ingenuity born in brutal conditions. For those of us who came of age under chronic stress, trauma, systemic oppression, or betrayal, survival wasn't just surviving. It was creating. Sculpting intricate armor to move through a world indifferent at best, hostile at worst.

For years, I wore my costumes expertly. I shifted language, demeanor, and ambitions to fit the context. To maximize acceptance and minimize danger. I was the scholar. The athlete. The leader. The dutiful son. Each role carried its own expectations and rewards. Each mask was a masterpiece of design, made for maximum survivability. But each came with a cost. A slow erosion of the self beneath the performance.

How Armor Forms Under Threat

From my earliest memories, the adaptations were underway. I was the "nice boy," a label that at first felt like simple acknowledgment of my nature. Later it would reveal itself as a deeply embedded survival strategy. To be seen as kind, affable, non-threatening wasn't just who I was. It was who I needed to be. Living in a country where Black boys were, and still are, often read first as threats, any deviation from harmlessness carried mortal risk. Every smile, every polished answer, every polite nod was part of the masterpiece I was constructing to ensure my survival.

The traumas that initiated these adaptations were not always grand or cinematic. More often, they were a thousand paper cuts. Betrayals of trust. Institutional gaslighting and subtle erasures of agency. I learned early there were dangers not just in outright violence but in emotional and psychological violations. My earliest traumas aged me before my time, robbing me of innocence others seemed to enjoy without question. It wasn't just that something happened. Something was taken. In its place, a complex system of survival plasticity was installed.

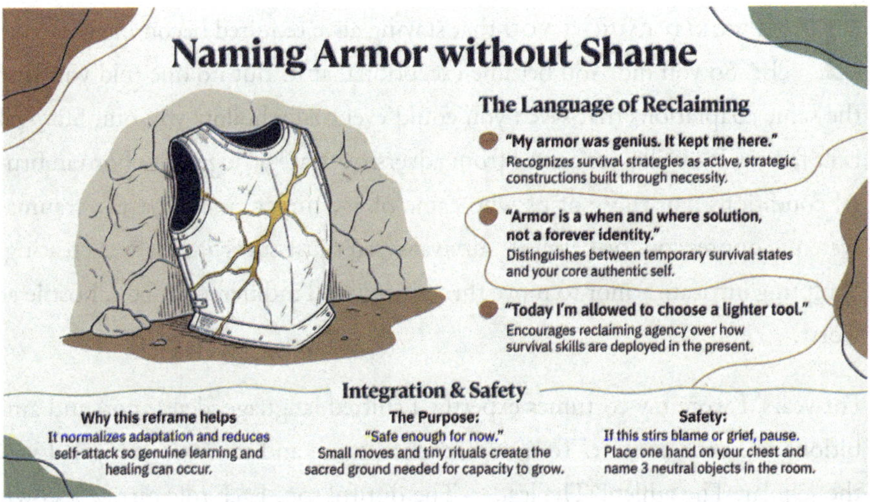

The Genius (and Limits) of Adaptation

Survival plasticity is the capacity of a person to mold oneself under extreme duress. Adapting behavior, thought processes, emotional expressions, and even physical presence to maximize safety. It's distinct from privilege plasticity, which is the capacity to mold and grow oneself within a secure, resourced environment. **Privilege plasticity** operates on the assumption of safety. Survival plasticity operates on the assumption of threat. One expands. The other constricts, refines, deflects, deceives – all in the service of remaining alive and intact.

What survival demands isn't what healing requires. Survival demanded a flexible yet durable, and often beautiful armor-like façade. Healing demands that we set down the armor and tend to the rawness beneath. But how does someone remove the armor when the world that demanded it remains unchanged? How do you risk the exposure of tender, reclaimed parts when you know, from experience, the cost of vulnerability?

This is the paradox we live with. The very adaptations that saved our lives can later limit them. The skills honed to art form under duress must eventually be reexamined, dismantled, reoriented toward flourishing rather than merely surviving. The greatest danger of mastery in survival is that it can be mistaken for thriving. From the outside, it often looks indistinguishable. The version of the self that can hold jobs, build families, lead communities, win accolades – all while managing, suppressing, or rechanneling the persistent undercurrents of fear, grief, and rage that were never given space to heal. But survival and thriving aren't synonyms. Survival is externally driven. Reactionary, often born of necessity. Thriving is internally directed. Creative, expansive, self-sustained. One protects life. The other builds it.

At some point, the survivor reaches a crossroads. The armor begins to chafe. The costumes, once lifesaving, become heavy, hot, and suffocating. The adaptations that felt like superpowers start to reveal their double edges. Hypervigilance becomes exhaustion. People-pleasing becomes resentment. Adaptability becomes erasure. The body, which has absorbed all these shifts in silence, eventually demands attention. Through fatigue, chronic pain, emotional numbness, or bursts of rage and despair.

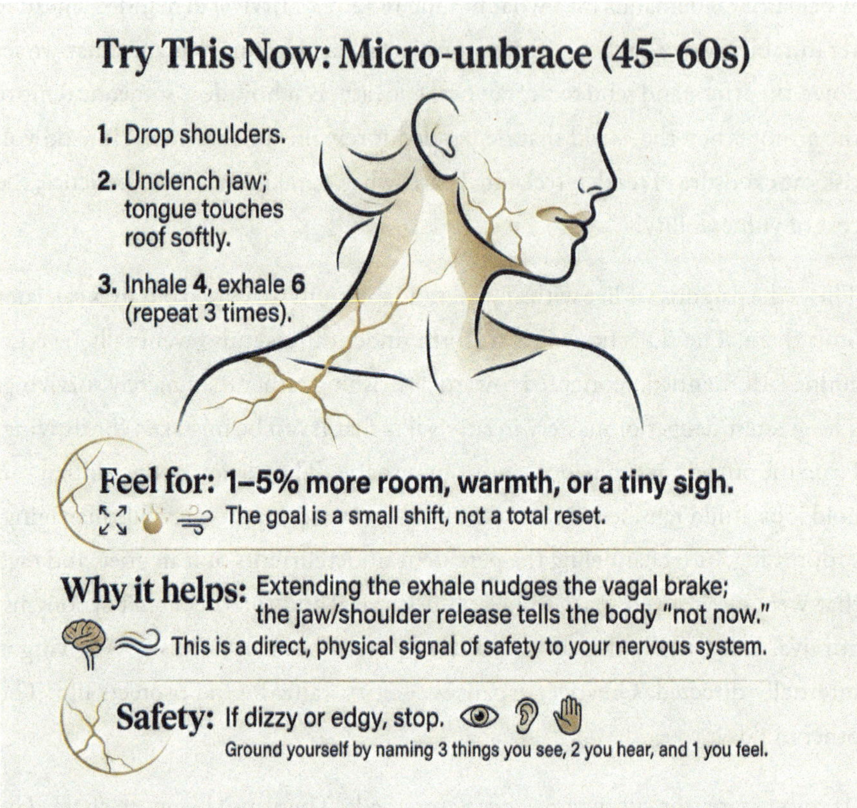

Birth of the Chameleon

There are two traumas from childhood I remember with brutal clarity. The first was on an overnight train from Greensboro, NC to New Orleans, LA. I was young. Small enough to still feel awe at the shape of the world out the window. Still trusting enough to believe the world would keep me safe while I slept. My mother sat across the aisle, asleep. I was playing a handheld Mattel football game, an obsession at the time. An anonymous man sat beside me. I can't tell you exactly what he did, but what I can tell you is the next thing I remember is the chaos. The shouting. Hands pulling me violently. Someone calling for the police. He vanished before anyone could stop him. They didn't catch him. I didn't even understand what had happened. I remember the crying and my body knowing something was wrong.

The second was closer to home – private, but no less damaging. A neighbor girl, two or three years older, decided to teach me about the birds and the bees in my parents' garage. When my father called for me, I instantly knew what we were doing was wrong. I hadn't even discovered myself yet. Hadn't developed the language or autonomy to consent, to comprehend, to resist. What I do remember is the shame and confusion. The sense that some internal line had been crossed without my permission.

These moments left me confused, betrayed, permanently aged. A boy still in the shell of a boy's body, but carrying a man's weariness in his chest. Those traumas installed an invisible but irreversible knowledge that something was coming for me. I couldn't name it then. But it would eventually crystallize into a truth that shaped my worldview. Survival was neither guaranteed nor benign. Violation and betrayal aged me. They cracked the thin lacquer of innocence that protects children from seeing the violence of the world too early. What was taken in those moments wasn't just safety. It was the ability to move through the world without a guard up.

Shame bloomed immediately after these traumas. Profound, paralyzing shame. Not merely the private shame of injury, but the public shame of being seen. Of knowing that others could glimpse, if only faintly, that something was broken in me. That the light in my eyes had dimmed. No amount of good grades or athletic trophies could restore it.

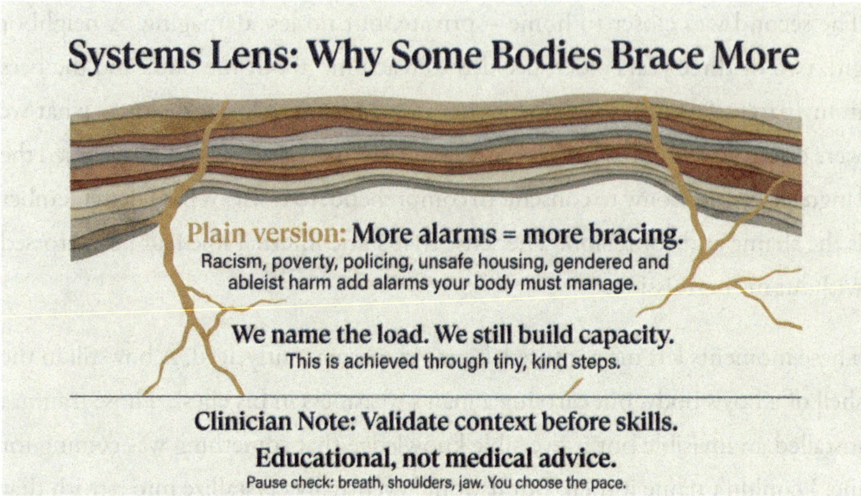

My very first mask rose from that fertile ground. The mask of "goodness." My first drug wasn't alcohol or anger. It was people-pleasing. I became a chameleon, shifting the pitch of my voice, the cadence of my speech, the vocabulary of my world to meet the needs and expectations of whatever room I entered. I absorbed cultures and customs with sponge-like hunger. I mastered the art of navigating every space with grace and affability, soothing and smoothing every potential conflict before it could erupt into open threat. I could walk through a Catholic school, a corporate boardroom, a martial arts dojo and in each space, become native without betraying the core self I fought to protect.

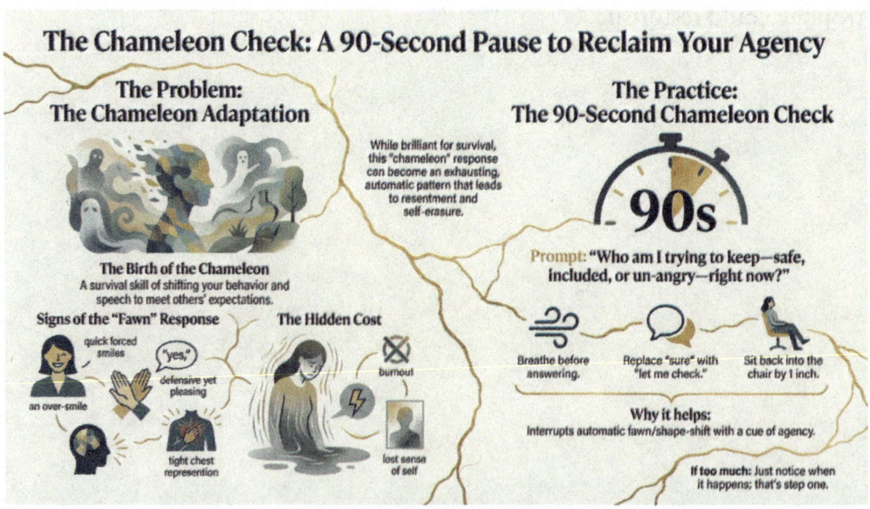

I never lost my original core. Somehow, through all of it, a spark of authenticity remained. A stubborn knowing that I was more than my adaptations. But the mask, the persona, became a second skin. It grew more elaborate with each passing year. Each new environment demanding new refinements. Yet, the deeper consequence of this constant chameleonic adaptation wasn't numbness. At least, not in the way most trauma survivors experience it. My survival did not manifest through dissociation or emotional freezing. It manifested through hyper-awareness.

I was a lifelong athlete involved in soccer, martial arts, tai chi, snowboarding, weightlifting, and my kinesthetic sense was sharp. I could feel the tension in a room before anyone spoke. Could sense danger in the shifting of weight in a stranger's body, in the slight delay before a smile. Could predict the next move in a conversation, sometimes finishing people's sentences internally before they could utter them aloud. I wasn't just moving through the world. I was scanning it constantly, running threat assessments at speeds even I couldn't always consciously track.

Hypervigilance became my superpower. I realized that if I could anticipate a person's need – emotional, physical, conversational – and address it before it surfaced, I could manage or even manipulate the interaction in ways that increased my probability of survival. I bent myself around expectations. Neutralized threats with charm and precision. Gave people what they needed to feel seen, heard, validated—often before they even consciously knew they needed it. In doing so, I bought myself safety. I told myself (still tell myself) to use these powers for good. To make the world easier, lighter, safer for others.

But this, too, had a cost. Each act of shapeshifting drained emotional currency from a finite reservoir. Each successful encounter was another torpedo absorbed by the plasma shields around my soul. Like any shield, it weakened under constant barrage.

When the trauma buffer overflowed and stress exceeded my available adaptive strategies, it manifested in risk-taking behaviors. My vice was primarily emotional eating. Craving cheap, sugary dopamine hits. I could always tell when I was nearing emotional bankruptcy because the cravings would rise like floodwaters: fast food, desserts, anything to distract and comfort the body that had carried me through yet another invisible battle.

Chinese medicine teaches that each emotion correlates to specific organ systems. Worry taxes the digestive system, leading to cravings for sweet foods. Sadness and grief weaken the lungs, evoking yearning for spicy or bitter flavors. Fear strains the kidneys, birthing cravings for salty foods. Anger targets the liver, inciting hunger for sourness. I've lived these truths viscerally. When my mind churns through endless threat assessments, my spleen and stomach scream for relief in the form of donuts and burgers. Not because I lack willpower. Because my body is trying to digest a world too heavy, too acidic, too relentless for normal metabolization.

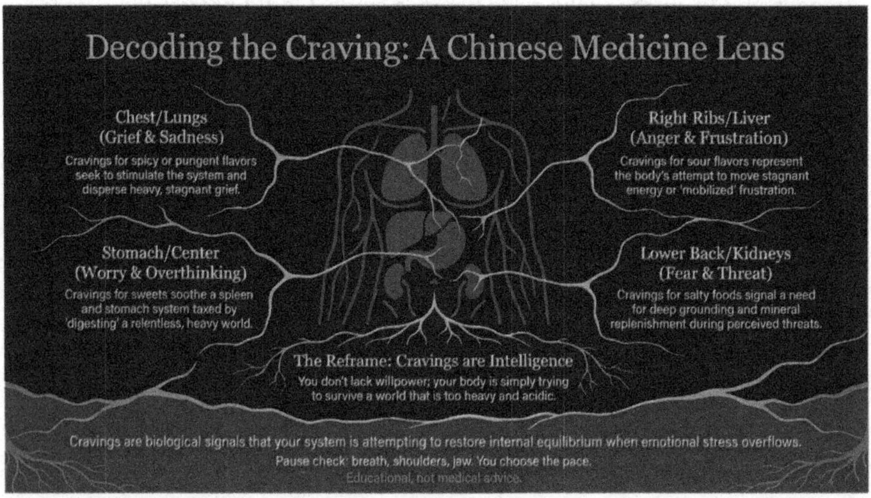

The emotional body and the physical body are not separate entities. They're symphonic instruments, vibrating together in grief and survival. Every adaptation I mastered, the kindness, the empathy, the prediction, the camouflage, exacted a toll my body carried in the background for decades. Shame built the first mask. Fear maintained it. Then, mastery of survival became its own prison.

Even within that prison, seeds of something else were sown. Seeds of inquiry. Seeds of defiance. A gnawing knowledge that survival wasn't the summit. That somewhere beyond the endlessly adapting chameleon, there might exist a version of myself not merely engineered for survival but sculpted for reclamation.

That hope, that furious, flickering hope, is why this book exists. Because somewhere, someone else feels it too. The vague, inchoate knowing that something is broken but refuses to die. This is not merely my story. It's the story of survival plasticity. It's the story of how trauma molds, disciplines, and weaponizes kindness and empathy into armor. It's the story of how against all odds some of us learn to use that armor not only to defend, but to heal. And eventually, to lay it down.

Patterns: Fight, Flight, Freeze, Fawn

In these early years, my body knew first what my mind hadn't yet learned words for. Tension patterns, hypervigilance, cravings for soothing foods, constant risk analysis – all emerged before I ever sat in a classroom discussing "fight, flight, freeze, or fawn." Before psychology named it, my body was living it. My survival masterpiece was encoded not only in my emotional habits but in my musculature, my breath patterns, my vigilance in new environments. Always scanning, adjusting, and surviving. These patterns are not flaws. They are the intelligent, automatic ways our bodies learn to keep us safe when the world feels unsafe.

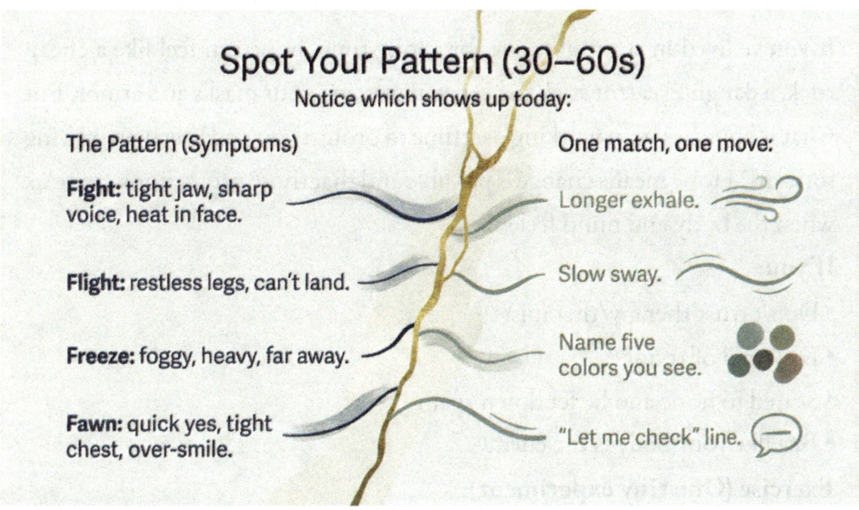

These patterns are not just personal quirks. They are echoes of how our communities have had to survive for generations. They show up in different ways, in different bodies, but the root is the same: a nervous system doing its best to protect itself from harm, shaped by the context of our lives.

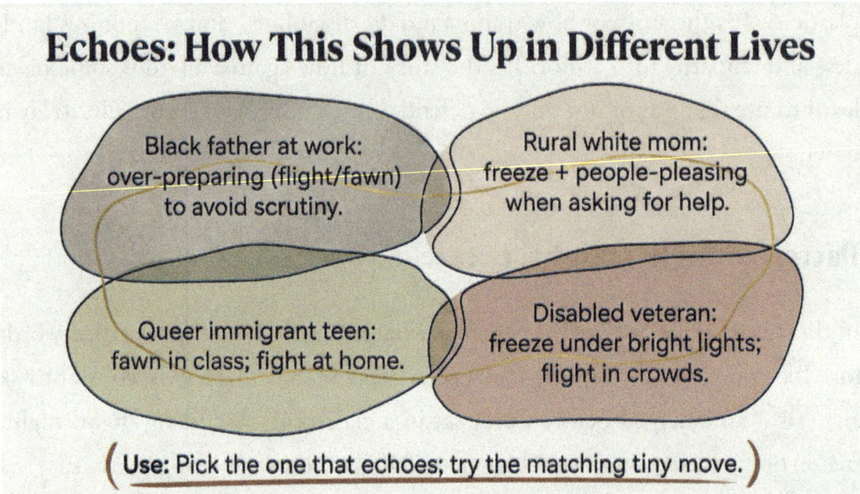

Hope that doesn't feel fake

If you've lived in survival mode for a long time, hope can feel like a cheap trick, a dangling carrot stick to keep you wearing your masks and armor. But what if hope has been working overtime to protect you and keep you moving forward? Hope means change is possible and that those protections can relax when the body and mind feel safe.

If you:

- Don't trust therapy/therapists
- Feel tired of trying
- Scared to hope and be let down again
- Feel like your body is the enemy

Exercise (One tiny experiment):

Without a mind to fix anything, once a day, ask yourself: "What are you trying to protect me from today?" Feel free to write the answer down, no wrong answers.

Hope Marker: Your Body Isn't the Enemy

The masterpiece of survival, no matter how finely crafted, was never meant to be a permanent home. It was meant to be a bridge. A temporary structure built in the midst of the flood. Its genius is undeniable. But living on it forever becomes a slow kind of torture. Recognizing the brilliance of our survival strategies is the first step toward reclaiming agency. These adaptations are not evidence of weakness or brokenness. They're proof of profound resilience and ingenuity. Monuments to the human spirit's refusal to be annihilated. Honoring them does not mean we must remain trapped within them.

In clinical terms, we must distinguish between adaptive functioning and expansive functioning. Adaptive functioning keeps the organism alive under adverse conditions. Expansive functioning allows for growth, creativity, and deeper relational connection. Trauma restricts the nervous system into perpetual adaptive states. Healing requires reactivating the capacity – the space – for flourishing.

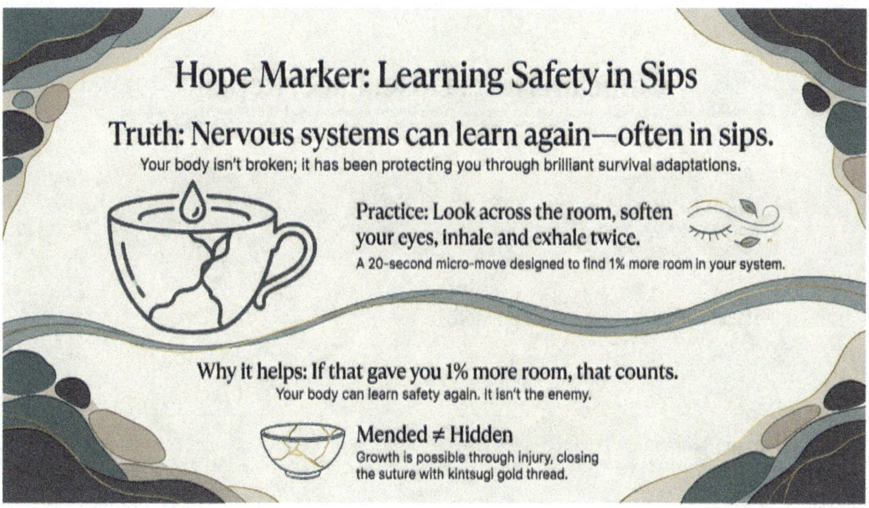

Weaponized survival occurs when systems, institutions, and cultural norms consistently demand that individuals remain in adaptive survival states to navigate their daily lives. It's not accidental. It's engineered by historical, political, and economic forces that rely on the suppression of certain groups' plasticity into permanent defensive modes. Recognizing this is critical, because if you believe your adaptations are personal failures, you are far less likely to challenge the systems that necessitated them.

Survival becomes a masterpiece of engineering under siege. But healing must become the masterpiece of peacetime, however fragile or brief that peace may seem. Healing is not forgetting the mask; it's learning when and how to set it down. Reclaiming the right to live without it when safety permits and fighting to build communities where more people can afford to take it off.

In this book, we will not romanticize survival. Nor will we vilify the armor, the masks, or the brilliant adaptations you may have needed to survive. We will recognize them as necessary, as ingenious, as powerful, and we will acknowledge that they are no longer enough for the life you are capable of living.

The journey back to you begins with this. Bowing in respect to the masterpiece you built under fire, then choosing, with open eyes and steady hands, to build something different. Not because you failed. Not because you were broken. But because you were always meant for more than survival alone.

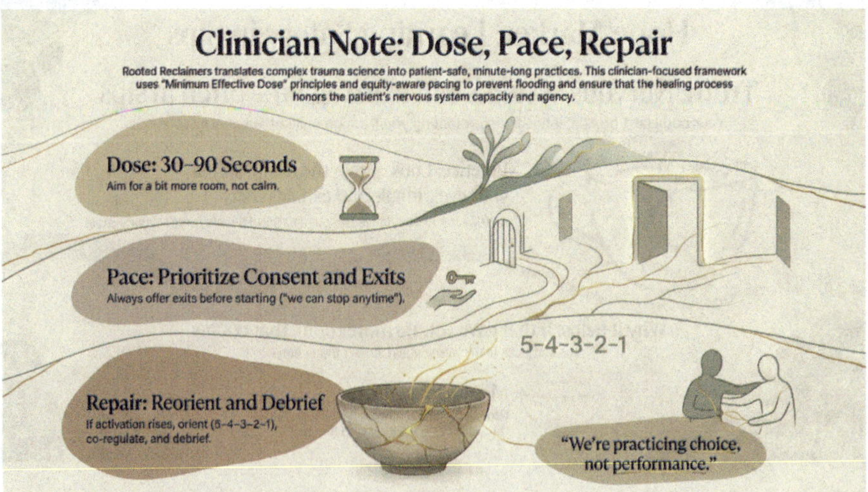

PART II

Cracks in the Armor

When the mask begins to slip.

Chapter 4

When Winning Still Feels Like Losing

In the mythology of survival, success is supposed to be the reward for all the suffering. From the time we're young, particularly in marginalized and working-class communities, we're taught that achievement is the way out. Get the degree. Win the promotion. Build the business. Escape the circumstances that once held you captive. Success becomes not just a goal but a moral mandate. A necessary justification for the pain endured along the way.

For many trauma survivors, especially those who grew up needing to constantly prove their worth, success becomes survival by another name. It becomes armor. If you are exceptional, no one can question your value. If you achieve enough, maybe the early betrayals, the unmet needs, the unspeakable griefs can be retroactively erased. Survival is no longer just about staying alive. It becomes about outperforming your past.

And sometimes, it works. On the surface, anyway.

The Overachievement Trap

You walk across the graduation stage. You shake the hand of a CEO. You see your name on an award. You buy the house, drive the car, accumulate the proof that you made it. To outsiders, you've become the embodiment of resilience, the living evidence that hard work and determination can overcome anything.

But there is a hidden story underneath the headlines of success. There is the hollow victory.

The reality is that if the early wounds remain unhealed, success doesn't fill the hole. It may cover it for a time, but it can't replace what was never nurtured in the first place. The applause fades quickly. The thrill of achievement wears off. And when the lights go down and the noise stops, you're left alone with yourself. Often for the first time.

This internal contradiction is often invisible to others. To the outside world, you're thriving. But inside, you're managing burnout, resentment, anxiety, or numbness. You feel the growing distance between the life you've built and the self that built it. And yet you keep going, because slowing down feels dangerous. If you stop winning, who will you be? If you stop performing, will the people around you stay?

Metrics Can't Regulate a Nervous System

The symptoms that once stayed dormant in the name of ambition now surface with force. Anxiety that won't be silenced by accomplishment. Depression that doesn't care how much you've achieved. Exhaustion that seeps deep into the bones despite all outward signs of triumph. Physical breakdowns – chronic illnesses, hypertension, cancer, autoimmune flares, pain syndromes – that seem to come "out of nowhere" but are, in fact, the body's long-delayed accounting.

This dissonance can be devastating. It's not only the loss of joy but the collapse of a survival strategy that has been operating for decades. If success was supposed to redeem the suffering, why does it still hurt after "winning"? Where do you go when the dreams turn hollow?

This moment is a critical inflection point in *journey from the edge*. It's where many trauma survivors either double down by chasing bigger victories, higher salaries, louder applause, or finally begin to confront the truth. No amount of external success can heal what was wounded internally.

Understanding the physiology behind this collapse is essential. Chronic survival activation, the nervous system being stuck in a state of hypervigilance, even while performing successfully, slowly wears down the body's regulatory systems. Cortisol and adrenaline, useful for short bursts of survival, become corrosive when elevated long-term. Inflammation rises. Immune system weakens. Sleep quality deteriorates. Emotional resilience frays. Over time, the body, unable to differentiate between the threat of poverty or abandonment and the pressure to "keep winning," treats both with the same stress response. Until it can no longer compensate.

The collapse often looks dramatic from the outside – a sudden health crisis, a mental health breakdown, a profound depression. Internally, it's the inevitable result of decades of cumulative, unresolved strain. Winning, in this context, didn't cause the breakdown. It simply removed the distraction that kept you from feeling what was always there.

Case Vignette: Gold Stars, Empty Body

Maria, age 23, looked like the overachieving high school senior, the first in her family to go to college. She is now sitting in her childhood bedroom, the diploma on her dresser. The house is quiet. But she is suffering from crippling anxiety, a deep dread that makes the air feel thick. She thinks about the suffering it took. The years of navigating a poor neighborhood, the grind, the constant fear of not being good enough.

Instead of relief, she feels crushing heaviness in her neck and shoulders, as if the diploma is the weight of the world.

The only thought that comes is this: "What is the next crucible I have to cross? What new gauntlet is waiting before I'm good enough just to survive, let alone thrive?"

This reckoning is painful but necessary. It forces the question that few survivors dare to ask during the climb. Who am I if I am not constantly achieving? Who am I without the next goal to chase?

The early lessons of survival taught us that rest was dangerous, that vulnerability was a liability, that stopping was death. In many families, cultures, and communities, rest meant falling even further behind. The tragedy is that we often internalized these lessons so deeply that even when the external threat lessened, the internal engine of overdrive never stopped.

To heal, you must grieve not only the pain but the mythology. You must grieve the version of yourself that believed achievement would heal the wound. You must grieve the years spent chasing enoughness. This isn't an act of self-betrayal. It's an act of reclamation.

Because real freedom, the kind that endures, is not found at the end of a resume or in the applause of a crowd. it's found in the slow, courageous, often agonizing work of becoming whole inside your own body, mind, and spirit.

Winning doesn't heal you. Healing heals you. And the road from hollow victories to self-reclamation begins when you are willing to stop running long enough to feel the cost of survival, and to choose something different. You choose something different because you are finally ready to live.

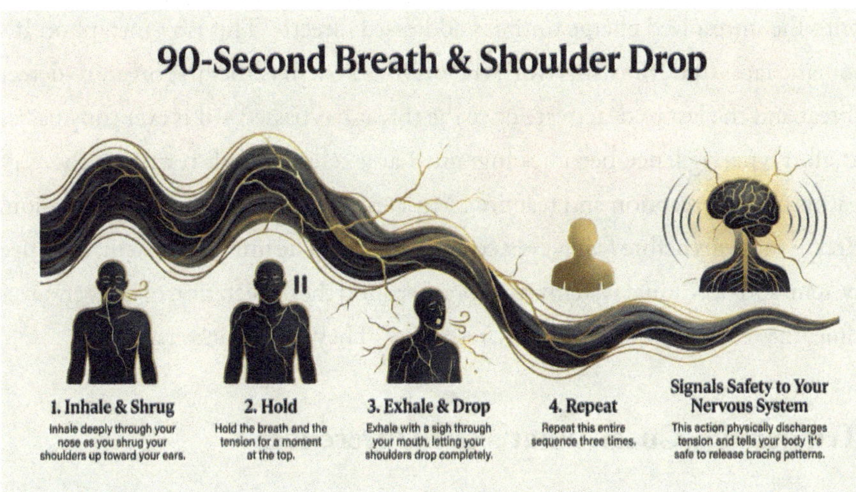

Chapter 5

The Body Remembers First

FOR A LONG TIME, many trauma survivors believe that if they can think their way past what happened, they can heal. If they can just understand it better, rationalize it, reframe it, or minimize it, they can move on. We cling to the idea that pain lives only in memory, only in the past, only in the mind.

Yet, trauma isn't just stored in stories we tell ourselves and others. Even if the conscious mind manages to reframe or bury a traumatic event, the body holds onto the unresolved charge until it's addressed directly. This isn't metaphor. It's somatic fact. In trauma survivors, the nervous system is the first organ to detect threat and the last to deactivate once the threat has passed – if it ever fully passes at all. Hypervigilance becomes ingrained at a cellular level, rewriting the very pathways of perception and reaction. Muscles tense without conscious decision. Breath shortens before fear is even consciously felt. The immune system, digestive system, and hormonal systems recalibrate around the expectation of danger. Over time, these adaptations cease to be responses. They harden into baselines.

Triggers vs. Cues: What's the Difference?

Many survivors only realize this when their physical health begins to deteriorate. Pain that once seemed occasional becomes chronic. Fatigue deepens into exhaustion that no amount of sleep resolves. Digestive issues, hormonal imbalances, autoimmune conditions like fibromyalgia, and nervous system dysregulation begin to surface. Seemingly without clear cause. Doctors may offer symptom management, but the underlying disruption often remains untreated because its true origin isn't purely biological. It's physiological, emotional, and historical all at once.

Understanding how this happens requires looking at the way the body is built to handle stress. The human organism is remarkably adaptive. In response to threat, real or perceived, the body mobilizes its survival systems. The sympathetic nervous system surges, muscles tense, heart rate accelerates, blood shunts to major muscle groups, and the brain sharpens its focus for immediate action. These adaptations are critical in life-or-death moments. They're also supposed to be temporary.

In a healthy cycle, once the threat passes, the body completes the stress response. The nervous system shifts back into parasympathetic dominance, rest, repair, digestion, and recovery. Muscles relax. Hormones rebalance. Memory consolidates. The organism returns to baseline.

But when trauma occurs, especially complex, chronic, or developmental trauma, the stress response doesn't complete. The body remains partially activated, trapped in a loop of unfinished survival energy. Over time, this unresolved activation reshapes the way the body operates at a fundamental level. Rewires how the nervous system evaluates safety. Reshapes posture, breathing patterns, digestion, immune function, even cellular regeneration.

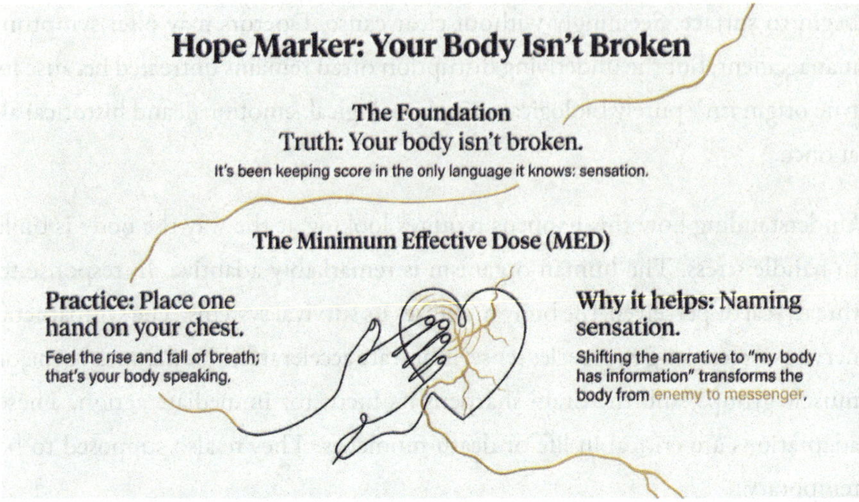

To use a practical analogy: imagine that every unresolved trauma is like an open application running in the background of your body's operating system. One or two minor apps may not slow the system down much. But over time, as more applications pile up – like ungrieved losses, unseen betrayals, unmanaged fear – the system becomes bogged down, sluggish, and vulnerable to crashing under even normal loads.

This physiological backlog explains why seemingly small stressors – disagreement at work, a minor injury, a bout of insomnia –can trigger outsized reactions in trauma survivors. Not weakness. Cumulative overload. The system is already taxed, and additional stress becomes the tipping point.

Autonomic States in Daily Life

The body's memory of trauma is often first expressed through symptoms long before it's understood cognitively. Some examples include a shoulder that stiffens inexplicably. A stomach that knots without clear cause. A digestive system in complete stagnation and constipation. A wave of fear or sadness that floods in response to an otherwise benign situation like a TV commercial or love song. These aren't random glitches. They're messages from the body's internal archive, signaling that something unresolved is demanding attention.

Modern neuroscience confirms what many ancient traditions have long known. Healing trauma requires engaging the body directly. Cognitive understanding is helpful, even essential for making meaning of what happened. But no amount of intellectual insight alone can discharge the stored survival energy trapped in the tissues. The body must be allowed to complete the cycles it was once forced to freeze. It must be invited, gently and safely, back into regulation. Contemporary research shows that being able to feel and sense what's happening inside the body is key to resolving trauma and helping the nervous system heal. Body-based therapies like sensorimotor psychotherapy have shown that real recovery often depends on including physical practices. Not just talk or insight.

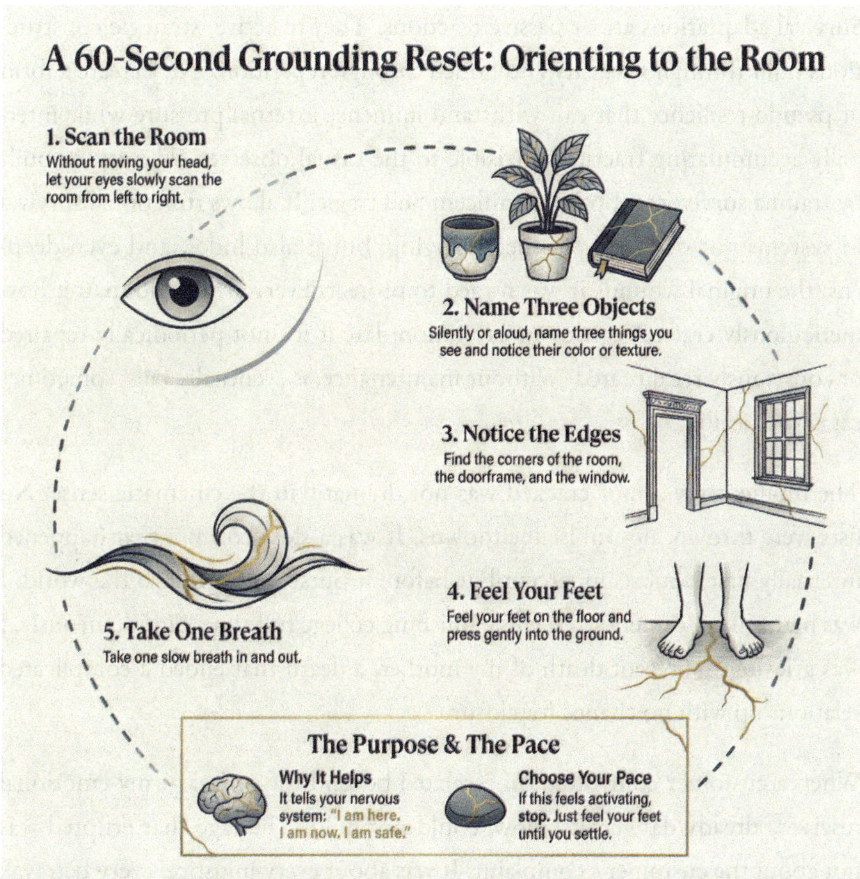

For many survivors, especially those whose bodies were sites of violence or betrayal, reconnecting with the body can feel terrifying. Dissociation, the mental disconnection from bodily sensation, becomes a survival strategy of its own. Breaking that pattern requires patience, safety, and trust. Often rebuilt inch by inch over months or years.

Healing the body's memory isn't about erasing what happened. It's about restoring choice. Re-teaching the body that not every touch is a threat, not every raised voice is danger, not every mistake will lead to abandonment. Making it safe, again, to inhabit yourself.

The Moment the Armor Cracked

Survival adaptations aren't passive reactions. They're active, strategic constructions built through necessity and honed through repetition. They create a form of pseudo-resilience that can withstand immense external pressure while internally accumulating fractures invisible to the casual observer. The armor built by trauma survivors is both magnificent and tragic. It allows functional survival in systems not designed for their thriving, but it also hides, and even deepens, the original wounds it was forged to protect. Every armor, no matter how meticulously crafted, carries an expiration date if it's not periodically repaired or consciously recalibrated. Without maintenance, it eventually fails, sometimes catastrophically.

The moment my armor cracked was not dramatic in the cinematic sense. No fists were thrown, no public meltdowns. It was a slow collapse that happened internally first, almost imperceptibly, before it burst outward into the world. I was managing a camera store while finishing college full time. Simultaneously, I was grieving the recent death of my mother, a death that ended a complicated relationship with no chance for closure.

When a customer confrontation escalated beyond the ordinary, my emotional reserves, already dangerously low, could not hold. The rage that erupted was not about the customer's complaint. It was about every injustice, every betrayal, every silencing I had ever experienced but had meticulously contained. My body responded before my mind could intercept. I felt the autonomic activation: heart rate surging, muscles primed, senses sharpening into combative hyperfocus. My vision tunneled. My mouth watered. I saw red, a phrase that until that moment had always sounded metaphorical. It was real. It was biochemical. It was survival mode stripped of diplomacy.

I verbally eviscerated the customer. I used my intelligence as a weapon, predicting his arguments before he could voice them and dismantling them with surgical precision. I humiliated him so thoroughly that he fled the store without filing a formal complaint. I "won" the battle. But inside, something sacred broke. Terry, my employee who witnessed the scene, looked at me with genuine fear and confusion. "Who are you right now?" they asked. It was a genuine question I couldn't answer. I didn't recognize myself either.

That moment was defining because in the act of winning the debate, I also lost part of myself. I grieved both the lack of control I exhibited, and how I'd shifted the focus of my anger from my personal life to someone who had nothing to do with any of it. Though I felt justified at the time, reflection sharpens with wisdom. When we don't take time to deconstruct our sharpest emotions, they tend to emerge at inappropriate times. It happens to all of us at one time or another.

If you've ever "won" and felt gross after

Let's not pretend that every victory is clean or righteous. If you read that & thought, "I've done that," then you're not alone. Winning can be a great way to feel safe, but it can also become an easy way to mask being wrong or avoiding important truths.

If you:

- Bully people in arguments when you feel cornered or know you are wrong
- Replay a fight later and feel genuinely bad about it
- Can't calm down, even long after it's over

Exercise (One tiny experiment):

If any of the above happen this week, ask yourself one question: "What do I gain, and what do I lose by winning this argument?"

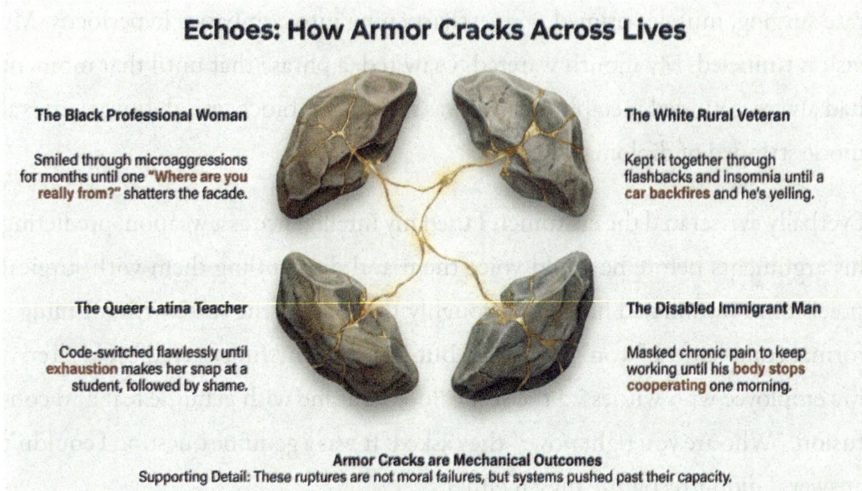

This moment also revealed something crucial about survival plasticity. The adaptations that make us high-functioning in trauma-saturated environments are the same ones that, under pressure, can become destructive. My gift of anticipatory empathy became a tool for calculated emotional violence. My leadership instinct mutated into domineering control. The very muscles that once maneuvered me through danger now turned on the world, and on myself. This is why survival skills must not be mistaken for true healing. They're provisional. They're inherently unstable once the trauma buffer becomes saturated.

The concept of **Unresolvable Trauma** crystallized for me during this period. Unresolvable trauma occurs when the source of injury, be it a person, institution, or historical legacy, is no longer accessible for confrontation, dialogue, or justice. The death of my mother removed any possibility of working through the complex, often painful dynamics that shaped our relationship. Her passing rendered the trauma unresolvable in the external world. All that remained was internal work: forgiveness of self, acceptance of permanent ambiguity, and the slow, brutal process of metabolizing pain without expectation of validation or closure.

Without conscious intervention, unresolvable trauma festers. It erodes internal structures of meaning, resilience, and self-trust. It compresses emotional space, shrinking the trauma buffer, and increasing the likelihood of armor failure under even moderate new stressors. Survivors of unresolvable trauma often oscillate between overperformance—trying to outrun the grief—and emotional collapse when the façade can no longer be sustained.

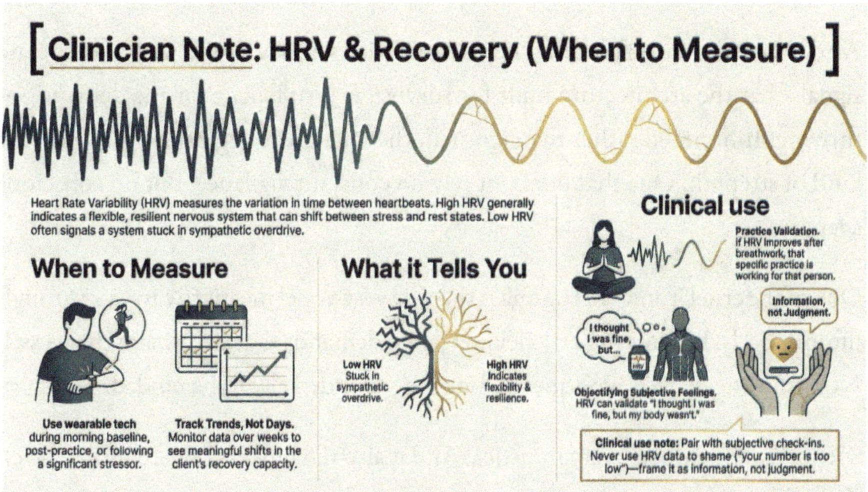

I've observed in my practice that the **Primary Coping Mechanism** predicts the nature of the **Trauma Spiral Reflex** under armor failure. Those who adapted through hypervigilance often collapse into rage or paranoia. Those who adapted through dissociation may plunge into numbing depression. Those who survived through people-pleasing may spiral into resentment or catastrophic self-betrayal. My spiral reflex was preemptive intellectual dominance. Anticipating threats and neutralizing them surgically. When destabilized, it transformed into strategic cruelty. A weaponization of empathy's shadow twin.

Understanding this predictable transformation was a revelation. It allowed me to shift from shame about the outburst to clinical curiosity about the mechanics behind it. I wasn't "broken" in a moral sense. I was broken in a systemic sense. I was overloaded, destabilized, and failed by adaptations that were brilliant in their original context but maladaptive now.

The work of self-reclamation requires first the recognition of these dynamics without judgment. To rebuild from the ruins of collapsed armor, we must become both the archaeologist and the architect. Excavating the true causes of collapse, then designing new structures capable of holding the weight of a more conscious, integrated existence. The goal is not to eliminate adaptive strengths like quick wit, strategic empathy, or situational leadership. It's to reclaim agency over when, why, and how they are deployed. To anchor them not in fear, but in freedom.

Armor cracks aren't failures. They're invitations. They're the body's desperate signals that the architecture built for survival is insufficient for the demands of thriving. If honored rather than ignored, they mark the beginning of a different kind of strength. One that does not rely on constant vigilance, but on conscious agency.

One of the cruel ironies of trauma is that the very vessel meant to carry us through life, our body, becomes a battlefield. Healing demands that we reclaim that vessel. Not as an enemy to be conquered, but as a wounded ally to be tended.

The body remembers every injustice. And it also remembers how to heal, if given the right conditions.

Relearning how to listen to those internal signals, telling you how to care for the body's needs, and how to restore its capacity for resilience and pleasure, is the beginning of true restoration. Not simply about symptom reduction. About reconnection with the body, the breath, and the deepest parts of the self that survival once demanded we abandon.

The journey home winds through the body first.

Not around it.

Not in spite of it.

Through it.

Pause check: breath, shoulders, jaw. You choose the pace.

Chapter 6

Silent Grief and Sacred Rage

GRIEF IS OFTEN THE first casualty of survival. If it has no outlet, it metastasizes. It doesn't dissolve with time. It doesn't lessen simply because the world demands that it be carried silently. Unexpressed grief becomes sacred not because it's holy, but because it becomes too vast, too dangerous, too transformative to be allowed into the public square. For survivors of profound trauma, grief is a companion so constant that its absence would feel unfamiliar. It's woven into the muscle memory of daily life, a background hum, demanding but largely unacknowledged.

There are layers to this grief. The grief for what was lost – the original violation, the betrayals, the stolen possibilities. The grief for the parts of the self that were amputated for survival. The grief for the relationships that could never fully flower because trust was a privilege too expensive to risk. And most heartbreakingly, there is the grief for the futures that were never allowed to materialize.

Grief: The Love That Lost Its Welcome

Grieving what might have been is its own category of loss. It's not simply sadness for opportunities missed. It's the visceral mourning of an alternate life path – one where plasticity could have been a tool of exploration rather than survival, one where the full range of human potential was available without the crushing weight of hypervigilance, code-switching, or emotional self-erasure. For many survivors, there is a multiversal grief. The grief for the versions of ourselves that could have existed in a world less poisoned by violence, betrayal, and systemic inequity.

This grief demands space, but the world we live in doesn't offer it freely, especially to certain bodies. Black grief, Indigenous grief, immigrant grief, queer grief – these are often viewed as threats, not wounds. Expression of sacred and justifiable rage in these groups is criminalized, pathologized, or dismissed. To grieve publicly while carrying the markings of a marginalized identity is to invite danger. The message is clear: mourn privately or not at all.

So many of us learn to grieve silently. We grieve in the spaces between responsibilities, in the early and late hours when the world is still, in the stolen moments when masks can slip without immediate consequence. We compartmentalize our grief, locking it away in the emotional closet, hoping that containment will make it manageable.

Silent grief does not vanish. It evolves. It often manifests as burnout, chronic depression, emotional numbness, persistent fatigue, or disconnection from joy. These symptoms are the residue of losses that were never properly grieved. When survivors begin the work of healing, they often discover that beneath their anger, exhaustion, or indifference lies an enormous well of unexpressed sorrow. Grief demands to be felt before it can be metabolized.

The Shackles of Shame

Shame is grief's evil twin. Grief says something precious was lost. Shame says *I was the reason it was taken*. It doesn't scream or burn. It blames and makes you small. Where grief pulls you toward mourning, shame keeps you from reaching at all. It teaches your body to pull back before connection even starts and leaves you vulnerable to another injury. What began as dodging rejection becomes so automatic it starts feeling like who you are.

Shame is often the bridge between what hurt you early on and how you move through the world now. It's the thing that stops the next sentence before it leaves your mouth because you don't think your voice matters. The filter that decides what's safe to show, for fear of either being seen too little or too much. The constant editor turning your real self into something more acceptable. It convinces your nervous system that being smaller, dimmer, and less visible is what keeps you safe. It happens because you learned exposure has a price. Your body remembers when standing out means getting hurt, and it adjusts.

While grief is doing its work, shame may take the opportunity to move in if the environment is right. It builds isolating walls where connection should be. You may even end up feeling alone inside relationships that look fine from the outside. When your body doesn't trust closeness anymore, it expects judgment in every look, and reads kindness as setup for disappointment. Shame doesn't just keep harm away. It keeps everything away.

Loosening shame happens slowly. It's not about forcing yourself to feel proud or confident. It's about catching yourself in the moments you want to disappear and choosing to stay anyway. Notice when your breath catches before speaking, or when your shoulders drop because someone really sees you. These small moments are where things start to shift. Every time you get attention and nothing bad happens, the pattern weakens a little. Each time you stay present instead of shrinking, you're building proof that being seen doesn't have to hurt.

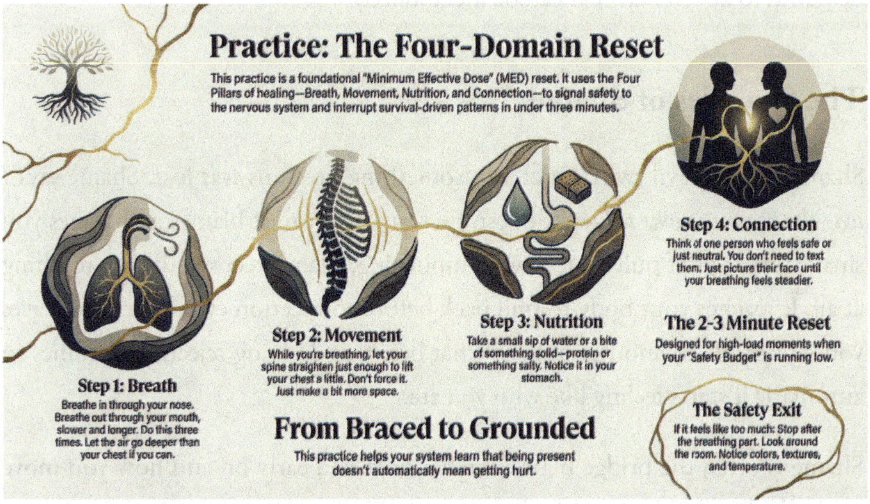

Shame starts to let go when your body learns it can be seen without something bad happening. You don't have to announce yourself or put on a show. You just stay present, moment by moment, without pulling back. When your nervous system stops treating visibility like danger, you naturally start taking up more space again.

That's what makes the next shift possible. Rage. Not the kind that tears things apart. The kind that draws a line. Rage is the boundary shame kept buried. It's the part of you saying, *I'm still here. I still matter.*

Rage: The Boundary That Arrived Late

Alongside silent grief is another force that many survivors are conditioned to suppress even more rigorously. Rage. Rage is a natural response to betrayal, violation, injustice, and helplessness. It's rooted in the body's defense systems, emerging as an instinctive attempt to protect the self when boundaries are crossed or dignity is assaulted. In a healthy context, rage signals that harm has occurred and that action must be taken to restore safety.

However, in environments where expressing anger is punished, ridiculed, or used as justification for further harm, rage becomes dangerous. Children who learn that anger invites violence or abandonment internalize the belief that feeling or showing rage is itself a threat to survival. Adults from marginalized communities often receive the same lesson through different mechanisms – penalized socially, economically, or legally for any display of justified anger.

Yet, anger is not the problem. Anger is a signal. It marks an unmet need or a violated boundary. When that signal is ignored long enough, the body escalates. Rage is escalation. Rage carries the force of months, years, and generations of dismissed protest.

Systems respond to rage by pathologizing it. They rarely address the unmet need that produced it. The body remembers both.

When rage cannot be safely expressed, it turns inward or leaks outward unpredictably. It may manifest as chronic muscle tension, autoimmune conditions, destructive self-criticism, high-risk or life-threatening behavior, or sudden emotional outbursts that feel disproportionate to the situation. In clinical terms, repressed rage can disrupt regulatory systems across the body and mind, creating a state of persistent internal conflict that exhausts resilience over time.

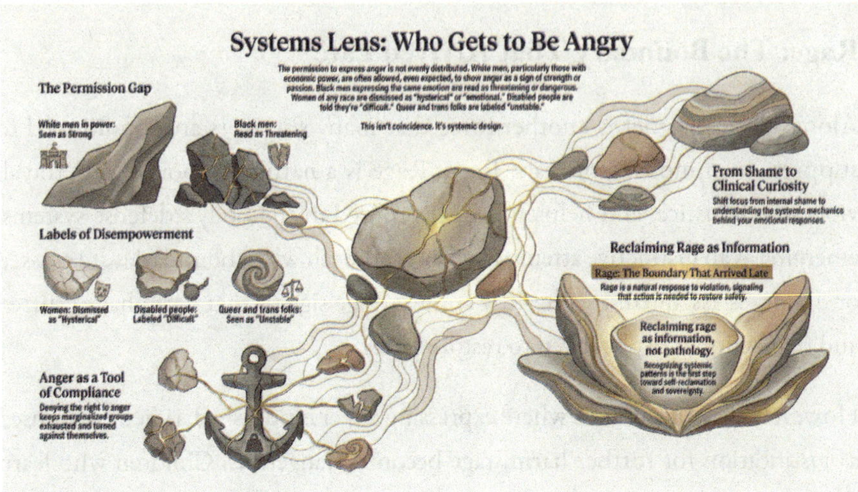

Systems Lens: Who Gets to Be Angry

The permission to express anger is not evenly distributed. White men, particularly those with economic power, are often allowed, even expected, to show anger as a sign of strength or passion. Black men expressing the same emotion are read as threatening or dangerous. Women of any race are dismissed as "hysterical" or "emotional." Disabled people are told they're "difficult." Queer and trans folks are labeled "unstable."

This isn't coincidence. It's systemic design. Denying certain groups the right to healthy anger keeps them compliant, exhausted, and turned against themselves. Recognizing this pattern is the first step toward reclaiming rage as information, not pathology.

Grief and rage are appropriate responses to violation, neglect, abandonment, and betrayal – not signs of dysfunction. They're the body's protest and the soul's resistance. Yet, in a society that pathologizes deep feelings and rewards emotional suppression, most of us learn early to hide these responses, especially if we were told, explicitly or implicitly, that our feelings made us unsafe, unlovable, or too much.

It's critical to understand that neither grief nor rage are moral failings. They are survival responses embedded in our human architecture. Treating them as problems to be eradicated only reinforces the original injury. Healing requires creating conditions where both grief and rage can be acknowledged, felt, and integrated without punishment or shame.

Grief provides access to mourning what was lost, clarifying the costs of survival. It softens defenses and allows the survivor to name the real impact of what they endured. Rage reestablishes boundaries that were once obliterated. It restores a sense of agency and defends the dignity that trauma sought to erase. Both are necessary. Neither can be skipped if the goal is true reclamation rather than cosmetic recovery.

When survivors attempt to heal without addressing their grief, they often build a fragile kind of functionality. They may appear successful or stable on the outside while internally remaining disconnected from their own emotional landscape. Without rage, survivors may develop deep insight into their pain but continue to allow new violations, unable to assert the basic boundaries required for sustained health.

The Event Horizon

There's a physics to grief. It has mass. It bends light. And when it reaches a certain density, when it has absorbed all it can hold without releasing, something shifts. Physicists call this an event horizon: the threshold of a black hole where all that consuming gravitational energy suddenly, violently transforms. What was pulling inward erupts outward in a torrent of creation.

That is what sacred rage is. It is grief reaching critical mass and exploding on the other side.

I know this not from a textbook but from a moment inside a moving car.

I'd been holding hope for someone I loved, a family member whose behavior had been wearing down my last reserves of patience for longer than I could honestly measure. The way you hold hope for people you are close to: gently, persistently, against mounting evidence. You keep believing they will choose differently. You absorb the small cruelties as the cost of proximity. You tell yourself that if you just remain steady, if you just stay kind enough and patient enough and present enough, the other person will eventually calm down.

But they didn't calm down. Instead, they crossed a line.

It was not the line itself that broke something open. It was the recognition, sudden and total, that I had spent enormous emotional currency on a debt that was never going to be paid. The grief of that realization coursing through me. And then it transformed.

The rage came up my spine like heat. My body was vibrating with adrenaline, but my voice, when it finally came, was controlled. I asked them to pull over, nicely. When they didn't, I said it again louder. When the car stopped, I told them plainly: "You do not get to tell me how to feel, how to conduct my personal relationships, or who I am allowed to love. I. Am. Done."

I walked away.

What I felt in that moment, standing outside the car, legs moving, chest a little more open, was something I had not felt before. Not triumph or relief. I was proud of myself. A version of me that had been waiting behind years of patience and accommodation stepped forward and claimed the ground it was always owed.

That was the event horizon. The grief had transformed.

Rage, when it arrives in this form, rooted in accumulated love and loss rather than impulsive reaction, isn't so much dangerous. It is clarifying. It redraws the boundary. It tells the mind and body: "We are no longer available for this." It restores the self-respect that the long patience of grief had slowly eroded.

The difference between sacred rage and reactive anger is the soil it grows from. Reactive anger is triggered. Sacred rage is earned. Reactive anger attacks the person. Sacred rage defends the principle. Reactive anger escalates. Sacred rage lands its punch, states its truth, and walks away.

Not every rage is sacred. But learning to recognize when your anger is actually grief that has found its feet is one of the most important distinctions on the healing journey.

If you have felt this before, that charged, clear, embodied moment when you stopped being patience and spoke the truth directly, you know what I mean. If you have not felt it yet, you may be still in the grief stage. That is fine. The event horizon arrives in its own time. You can't force it. You create the conditions.

Grief and Rage are not "bad" emotions. They're just drawn that way.

I'll say it like this: if you've been holding it together for years and your frustration has hit critical mass, your anger makes sense, your sadness and grief make sense, your rage makes sense. These emotions are tethered to the human experience. They protect and soothe, comfort and repel, process and discharge. They are proof that you are living the full range of humanity.

If you:

- Cry in private and are stoic in public
- Feel numb and can't access your tears anywhere
- Feel guilty for expressing any emotions

Exercise (One tiny experiment):

As one of your named emotions comes up, place one hand on the chest and one hand on the belly. Say to yourself, without judgement, "This is ___ (rage, grief, worry, sadness, fear). You are ok to be here. Thank you for protecting me."

When Survival Strategies Stopped Working

Every adaptation has a shelf life. What once preserves life eventually distorts it. This is a fundamental law not only of trauma psychology but of every living system under evolutionary pressure. When an organism's survival strategies no longer serve its environment, they either mutate, become maladaptive, or initiate the organism's collapse. Trauma survivors live at this evolutionary brink for years, sometimes decades. Refining, modifying, upgrading their adaptations until those very adaptations become the architects of burnout, disillusionment, and existential exhaustion.

I built an extraordinary life out of survival adaptations. I became exceptional at reading rooms, preemptively solving problems, leading movements without being perceived as a threat, and intuitively giving people exactly what they needed to feel safe, seen, and satisfied. Leadership became my natural habitat. Not out of ambition, but because leadership abhors a vacuum, and survival demanded that I stay near the control panels of every system I entered. The deeper truth was that I needed leadership as a defensive adaptation. It allowed me to guide the chaos rather than be consumed by it.

People respond to this kind of mastery with admiration, accolades, promotions, and even reverence. But none of those external affirmations rewired the internal architecture still being managed by my earliest, trauma-born algorithms. No award, no degree, no speech could change the fact that my success was built, in part, to outrun the deeper griefs and injuries never metabolized. My mask had simply become more elaborate. More socially celebrated. But it was still a mask.

When survival adaptations begin to fail, they do so quietly at first. Fatigue deepens. Joy evaporates. Relationships thin or collapse under the weight of unspoken expectations. Internal narratives become harsher and more rigid. The same strategies that once secured survival now paradoxically erode quality of life. The effort required to maintain appearances skyrockets, while the perceived rewards diminish. The trauma buffer saturates silently. When it fails, it often fails catastrophically.

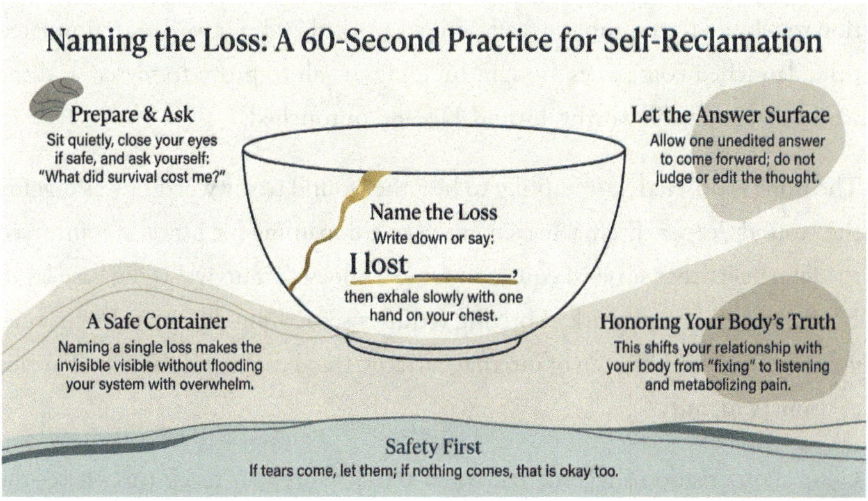

My rupture came in my late 30s. A workplace conflict, minor by itself, cascaded into a complete implosion of a professional identity I'd spent decades curating. I was fired. Not politely. Not with understanding. I was dismissed swiftly under a zero-tolerance policy, a scapegoat offered to institutional reputation management. All the letters, the appeals, the character witnesses could not save me. And that, precisely, was the trauma trigger. The realization that all of my brilliance, all of my survival engineering, could not ultimately save me from the vulnerability of being human.

The firing shattered my internal mythology. I had constructed my identity around being beyond reproach. A good man, a principled leader, a master navigator of conflict. In one fell swoop, that identity was compromised. No longer could I claim unblemished professional integrity. The trauma spiral reflex activated immediately. Rationalization, self-blame, minimization, externalization. Anything to prevent the deeper existential collapse of having to admit that I was not invincible. That I could fail. That I could bleed.

Survival plasticity had gotten me this far. But survival plasticity had no blueprint for what to do when the external validation that had become my emotional scaffolding was stripped away. And so, I did what many trauma survivors do after catastrophic adaptation failure. I overcorrected. I doubled down on achievement. I pursued new degrees, new certifications, new accolades with a feverish desperation to rebuild the crumbling scaffolding. I worked 70-hour weeks, accumulated titles, launched companies, bought buildings – all to prove to myself and the world that I was still worthy, formidable, and untouched.

The irony is brutal. In attempting to heal the wound to my worth, I was digging the wound deeper. Each achievement gave a dopamine hit but also reinforced the false belief that survival equals thriving. It doesn't. Survival is the base layer. It's the skeletal framework. Thriving requires something different. Intentional vulnerability, recalibration of internal narratives, and the abandonment of armor as primary identity.

Clinical observation suggests that when trauma survivors reach this phase–the failure of survival adaptations–they have three pathways. Collapse, dissociation, or transformation. Collapse manifests as depression, addiction, nihilism. Dissociation manifests as emotional numbing, apathy, resignation. Transformation is the rarest path, and the hardest. It requires facing the wreckage of the adaptations with radical honesty and choosing to rebuild an identity not rooted in defensiveness but in agency.

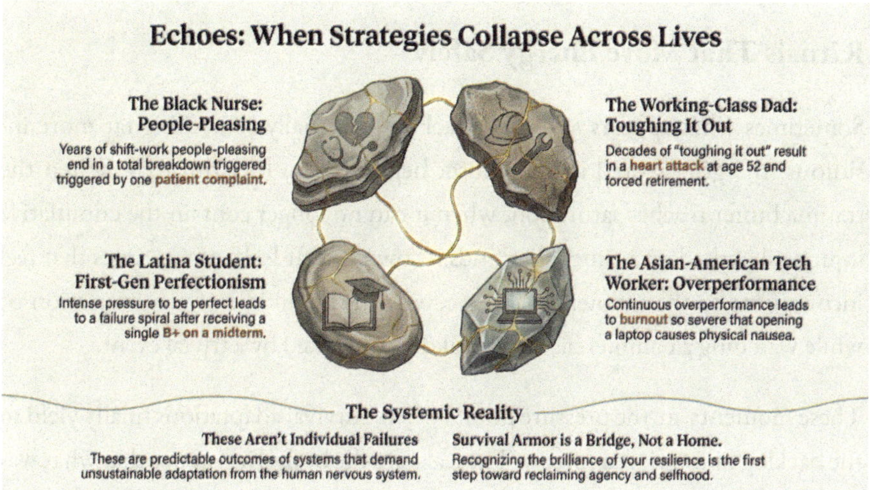

Through this process, I came to formulate one of the major hypotheses of this book. When new trauma matches the archetype of original trauma, its impact is not additive, but multiplicative. Being fired, rejected, shamed, cast out wasn't merely about the job. It activated the early shame of childhood betrayals, the primal wound of not being safe, of not being good enough to protect myself from harm. The emotional charge was exponential. Every unprocessed shame-based trauma in the system was suddenly vibrating, reanimated.

Recognizing this dynamic allowed me to begin a different kind of work. I stopped trying to escape the wreckage. I started sifting through it, naming each piece, honoring its history, grieving its necessity, and letting go of what no longer served. This is the slow, incredibly important work of reclamation. Not pretending the armor never existed or that the mask was a lie. But choosing, consciously, what to carry forward and what to lay down.

Evolutionarily, survival strategies were built for battle conditions and emergency navigation. They were designed for triage and stopped working because they were never designed for full-spectrum human flourishing. When the war quiets or when the survivor realizes they can't live forever as a ghost wandering the battlefield, the work must change.

Rituals That Move Energy Safely

Sometimes what appears as armor cracking is actually something far more insidious: the grief stored in the Closet beginning to leak through. When the trauma buffer reaches saturation, when it can no longer contain the cumulative injuries absorbed over time, grief finds its own exit. It leaks out at times that feel incongruent to the moment. Like, weeping in the middle of a conversation or while watching a commercial or a breakdown sparked by a trivial event.

These moments are the pressure points where survival adaptations finally yield to the backlog of ungrieved sorrow. The leaks are the body's insistence that what was buried will eventually search for the light.

The work of reclaiming grief and rage is methodical. It's rarely dramatic. It requires moving at a pace the nervous system can tolerate, gradually expanding the capacity to feel without becoming overwhelmed. It varies person to person but may involve:

Grief rituals: They vary by culture including *Sitting Shiva*, "Letting Go" ceremonies, memory quilts, collaborative art, and offer both containment (safe, bounded expression) and connection (community, ancestors, and nature). Grief rituals are found in almost every culture, even being found in pop culture in the pouring out of liquid for a fallen ally.

Somatic therapies, including mindful movement and Breathwork like yoga, Tai Chi, and Qigong, Somatic Experiencing (SE) by Peter Levine, and Somatic Rituals found in Indigenous communities, externalize internal distress, helping to release trauma rather than staying stuck in cognitive loops. These therapies create space to reintegrate body and breath, and space to move through mental and emotional stagnation.

Other community tools include things like community acupuncture, group therapy, assertiveness training, and community support structures that normalize rather than stigmatize these.

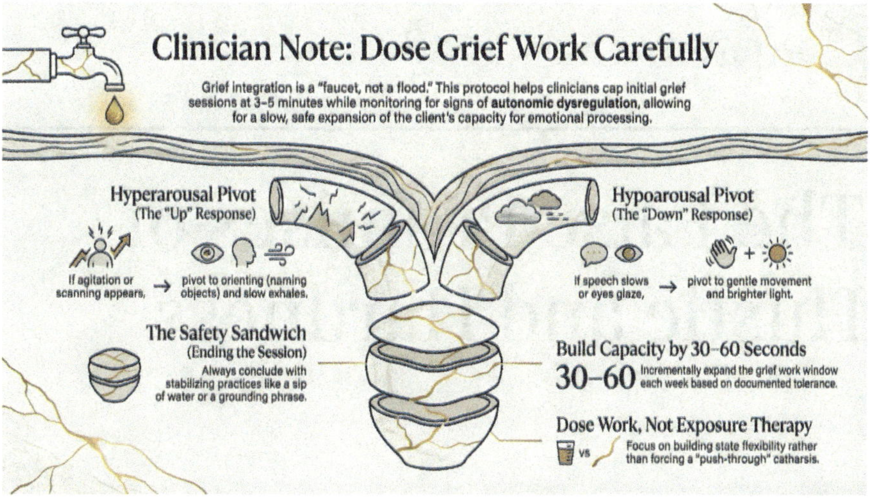

Old grief can surface suddenly after years of silence. Rage may erupt after decades of suppression, seemingly triggered by a minor incident but rooted in a history of unacknowledged harms. The task isn't to suppress or sanitize these reactions but to meet them with structure, containment, and respect.

Healing in this way does not mean glorifying suffering or wallowing in anger. It means honoring the biological truth that both grief and rage are survival intelligence at work. They're signals that the self was wounded and that the wound still matters. Healing transforms grief from a secret ache into a source of wisdom. It transforms rage from a destabilizing force into a focused, protective energy.

Learning to carry grief and rage without becoming imprisoned by them is a major milestone on the journey home. It allows the survivor to inhabit a wider emotional range, to reclaim parts of themselves that were once exiled for safety's sake. It opens the possibility of living not merely in reaction to the past but in genuine relationship with the present.

Grief names what was lost. Rage defends what remains. Together, they create the conditions for rebuilding a life that isn't governed by survival alone but infused with sovereignty, depth, and choice.

It's not a betrayal of the past self to change. It's the highest form of loyalty to the original dream. Finally, to live – fully.

Chapter 7

The False Promises of Hustle and Hardness

Cultures steeped in survival plasticity often worship two false gods: hustle and hardness. These ideals are sold as virtues, but they're often camouflage for chronic trauma responses. In communities where resources are scarce, discrimination is systemic, and safety isn't guaranteed, relentless work and emotional invulnerability aren't framed as choices. They're framed as necessities.

From a young age, many trauma survivors are taught, explicitly or through observation, that resting is lazy, asking for help is weakness, and softness is dangerous. Strength is defined not by the ability to adapt fluidly but by the ability to endure, to push through, to grind past exhaustion, injury, and even illness.

Productivity as Distraction

Work becomes a survival strategy. Busyness becomes a shield against despair. Toughness becomes a substitute for safety.

At first, hustle and hardness seem to pay dividends. They offer external rewards – better jobs, more money, social validation, and temporary distance from the circumstances that originally demanded survival at all costs. They create the illusion of control over an unpredictable world. If you can outwork everyone around you, perhaps you can outrun the consequences of being vulnerable.

The body and the spirit have limits that ideology cannot erase. Chronic overwork floods the nervous system with sustained stress hormones, degrading immune function, impairing cognitive flexibility, and increasing susceptibility to chronic illnesses. Emotional hardness, while useful in the short term, gradually disconnects the individual from authentic emotional signaling, making it difficult to recognize when a situation is unsafe, unjust, or unsustainable. In frank terms, this is not just a dissociation from traumatic memories, but from present-moment needs.

Hustle and hardness mask the underlying damage until the system begins to break down. Sleep becomes fragmented. Focus deteriorates. Relationships erode under the weight of emotional unavailability. Bodies develop syndromes and dysfunctions that defy simple medical explanations. By the time most survivors realize that hustle and hardness have stopped serving them, the damage is already well advanced.

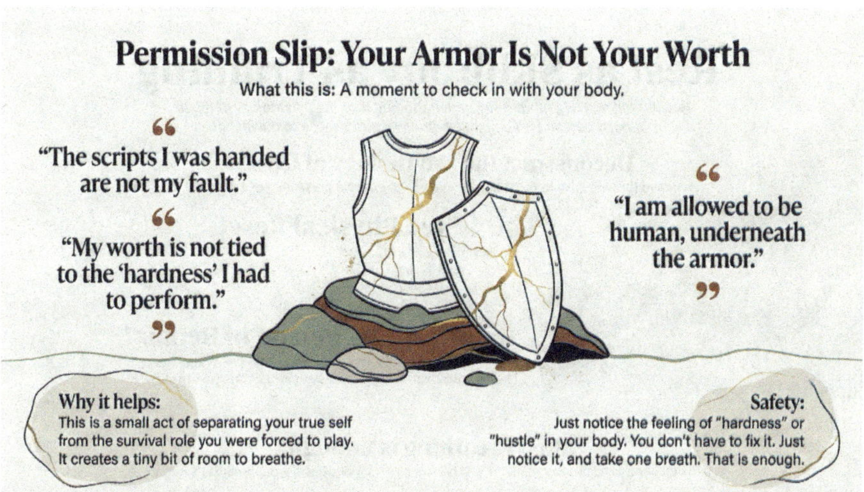

Masculinity/Respectability Scripts & the Body

The pressure to hustle isn't always felt equally. It's often tied to the scripts and tropes we're handed about who we're supposed to be in our society.

Society tells men they have lost their edge, that they must regain "manliness." This is often a call for toxic stoicism, a "hardness" that is unhealthy for any man. Outdated ideas still tell a man his worth is tied to his ability to lead and support a household. This is an unfortunate state to be in. Men are working harder than ever. For the first time in generations, many have less to show for it than their parents.

This hardness and hustle become a sacrificial contract. Men are asked to trade their full human experience. They sacrifice emotional range, empathy, and softness. In exchange, they're promised a spot in a fragile power structure, one that sustains itself even at its own peril.

This is the cost of conforming to the "status quo." It's a socioeconomic issue, not just a racial one. Anyone outside that narrow mold must sacrifice parts of themselves to fit. It's an unnatural fit. It requires canceling the parts of you that are real, just to belong.

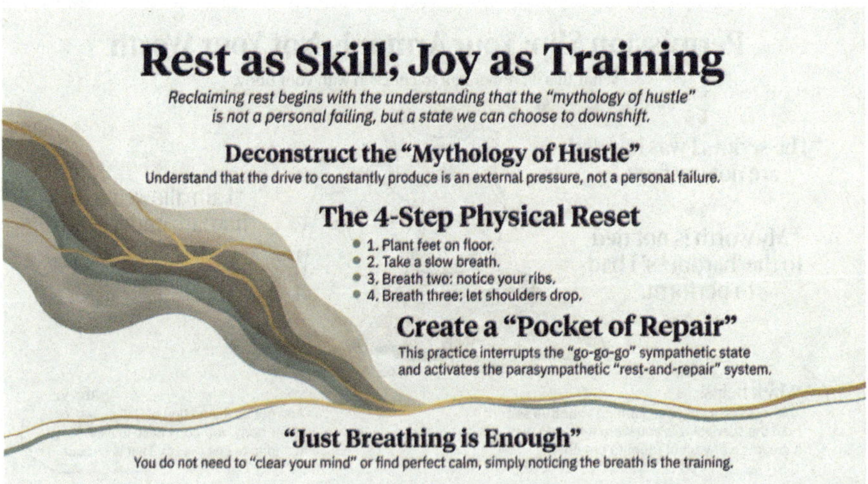

Unlearning the worship of hustle and hardness often triggers deep existential fear for trauma survivors. If you aren't constantly achieving, who are you? If you allow yourself to feel, will you fall apart? If you stop pushing, will the world crush you? These fears are not irrational. They were learned through real experiences of scarcity, abandonment, and betrayal. They must be honored even as they are challenged.

Healing requires building new internal architectures of safety that don't depend on exhaustion or numbness. This often involves learning to recognize early signs of stress and overwhelm, setting boundaries that prioritize recovery over appearance, and tolerating the discomfort of rest without compulsively reaching for distraction or new projects.

One of the most painful realizations in this phase of recovery is that not all relationships, workplaces, or communities will support this shift. Some are invested in your hustle and hardness because it serves their interests. Some will interpret your slowing down, your softening, as a threat or betrayal. Navigating this reality requires courage and clarity – often a period of profound loneliness – before new, healthier connections can be formed.

Context & Systems: Work, Policing, and Chronic Threat

The pressure of work is only one part of the story. This chronic threat is magnified by the systems we live in. The daily, low-grade hum of navigating racism, sexism, or classism drains the trauma buffer. The threat of aggressive policing in some neighborhoods, or the fear of economic collapse in others, is a constant weight.

These are not small things. They are societal burdens. They demand hustle and hardness from the body just to get through the day, long before you ever clock in at a job.

Ultimately, the false promises of hustle and hardness are exposed by the simple truth that no one can outrun the human need for care, connection, and rest. No amount of work can fill the space where nurturing was denied. No amount of toughness can protect against the physiological collapse that chronic survival mode inevitably creates.

Choosing to step off the treadmill of endless hustle isn't an abdication of responsibility. It's an act of self-reclamation – the refusal to sacrifice the rest of your life on the altar of survival adaptations that no longer serve your highest good.

The journey demands that you surrender the illusions that work is worth more than wellness and that toughness is the same as health. It demands you redefine strength – not as the ability to carry unbearable loads forever, but as the wisdom to lay them down when they are crushing the very life you are trying to protect.

The journey asks you to trade exhaustion for aliveness, performance for presence, and survival for sovereignty.

You were not made only to hustle. You were not built only to harden. You were made to live. Free, fully, deeply, and unapologetically.

If hustle has been your religion, it was mine for years as well.

Hustle has been the major force in many of our lives. It has paid our bills, earned us respect, and helped us feel safe. But when you are exhausted all the time and constantly chasing the next thing, your body waves a bright caution flag. It's trying to save you, not judge you.

If you:

- Don't know who you are outside of the "hustle"
- Keep pushing even when you are sick or recovering
- Feel behind no matter how much you accomplish

Exercise (One tiny experiment):

Slow down. Pick a day and choose to do one action item that normally stresses you out. Slow down on the task 20%. Each time you slow down, you signal to your brain that rest is not the enemy.

PART III

The Privilege of Plasticity

Where the light enters in.

Chapter 8

The Illusion and Possibility of Freedom

PLASTICITY, IN ITS PUREST form, is a dynamic state of continuous adjustment, growth, and adaptation. It's never idle. In any environment, the plasticity of the human being is either building toward expansion – what I term privilege plasticity, or condensing for survival – what I term survival plasticity. There's no neutral gear. There's no resting state. Our systems are responding, minute by minute, to the degree of freedom or oppression present in the surrounding environment. Whether we consciously recognize it or not, our bodies and minds are always adapting either to maximize potential or to minimize risk.

Freedom, as an existential and sociological concept, is therefore not a passive condition. It's active. It must be maintained, exercised, and protected. True freedom requires more than the absence of immediate threat. It demands the presence of sustained safety, opportunity, and recognition – not merely for individuals but for communities.

If you can't relax, that's OK for now, too.

Sometimes systems are wired to the "on" position like a light switch. These systems have been trained to stay active. We have to teach them how to deactivate, though not by force, but by giving them small examples of safety.

If you:

- Feel more stressed on a day off
- Find yourself scanning the room, even in "safe" places
- Sleep all night and still wake up tired

Exercise (One tiny experiment):

Once per day, do a 20-30 second self-check-in. Notice your feet on the floor, your chest and abdomen expanding and contracting with each breath. Notice where your shoulders are and any tension you are holding. Use each breath during the self-check in to relax one or two body parts.

Conditional Safety vs. Freedom

In that sense, much of what we call "freedom" in survival-dominant societies is a carefully curated illusion. We're often free only to the degree that we are able to navigate the restrictions imposed upon us without triggering punishment, isolation, or violence.

The trauma survivor understands this implicitly. For those of us who grew up in environments that demanded constant vigilance, freedom has often been a mirage shimmering just out of reach. It's a word sewn into national anthems and scrawled on monuments, but it doesn't live easily in the body. Instead, what lives in the body is the calculation of how far one can stretch before risking collapse. It's not the expansion of freedom but the flexibility of the trauma buffer that determines survival. Thus, plasticity born of survival is both a triumph and a tragedy.

Privilege plasticity is fundamentally different. Privilege plasticity assumes a starting point of safety, or at minimum, a baseline expectation of benevolence from the external world. It assumes that mistakes can be survivable, that missteps are opportunities for growth rather than triggers for catastrophic consequence. Privilege plasticity allows experimentation, creativity, curiosity, future planning, and play, which are the essential ingredients for profound cognitive, emotional, and existential development. It allows the nervous system to calibrate not only for defense but for connection, innovation, and thriving.

In contrast, survival plasticity is about minimizing damage. It sharpens the nervous system into a tool for predicting threats and avoiding annihilation. It privileges short-term risk calculations over long-term creativity. It trains the mind toward hypervigilance rather than exploration. It conditions the spirit to measure self-worth against the arbitrary metrics of external control systems: Am I safe today? Am I pleasing enough to be spared? Am I invisible enough to escape notice?

This is a living, breathing reality that manifests across every stratum of human society. It shapes how we parent, how we educate, how we govern, and how we dream – or fail to dream at all. In marginalized communities, the cost of survival plasticity is paid generationally. It's embedded in genetic expressions, stress reactivity profiles, and the intergenerational transmission of trauma that recalibrates the very architecture of human potential. This is more than metaphor. It's biology, neurology, and sociology in concert, playing a tune for the lost possibilities.

Micro-Liberties: Practicing Choice

It's important to recognize that no one is fully immune from survival plasticity. Even those born into relative safety can be thrust into survival modes by personal, familial, or societal upheavals. But the difference lies in the ability to return to a baseline of neuroplastic potential, where the brain can choose once again between survival or privilege and find safe harbor quickly enough that the body does not have to harden permanently against the world.

For many trauma survivors, especially those from historically marginalized communities, there's no baseline to return to. There‘s only the hardening, the vigilance, the constant recalibration toward threat management. This has profound implications not just for individual healing but for societal evolution. If entire populations are locked into survival plasticity, their collective cognitive, creative, and connective potentials are suppressed. This isn't just a tragedy for the individuals involved; it's a profound loss for humanity.

Thus, when we speak of reclamation, we are not speaking solely of individual therapy or personal growth. We are speaking of systemic disruption, of creating environments that foster privilege plasticity where survival plasticity once reigned. These spaces look like meeting places where dialog and movement are encouraged and facilitated. We are talking about curating and expanding our trauma buffer not merely through personal willpower but through collective, communal, and structural change.

The illusion of freedom is seductive because it offers the promise of autonomy without requiring the dismantling of oppressive systems. The possibility of freedom – real freedom – demands more. It demands that we see survival plasticity not as a personal failing but as a predictable consequence of hostile environments. It demands that we recognize privilege plasticity not as a reward for virtue but as the default birthright of every human being.

Try This Now: One "Unnecessary" 30-Second Pause

1. **Stop what you are doing.** Sometime today, for no reason at all, just stop.
2. **Change your view.** Stand up or simply look out the window.
3. **Take one slow breath.** Do nothing productive for 30 full seconds—and do not check your phone.
4. **Claim your "tiny sip of freedom."** This is a safe act of defiance against the internal pressure to always be producing.

Why it helps: This is a small, safe act of defiance against "internalized policing." It teaches your nervous system that you are allowed to exist without being productive, that you can claim time just for yourself.

Safety: If this feels agitating, that's okay. It's just data. Try 30 seconds tomorrow.

There's no shame in recognizing how far from freedom many of us have been forced to live. James Baldwin once said, "Freedom is not something that anybody can be given. Freedom is something people take, and people are as free as they want to be."

There's no shame in naming the longing for more. What matters is the work we choose to do with that recognition. The slow, steady construction of lives, communities, and systems where privilege plasticity is not the rare exception but the common ground.

Freedom, then, is not a destination. It's a practice. A decision made daily, hourly, minute by minute, to reclaim one's right to expand, to explore, to evolve without fear of annihilation. It's the sacred labor of the Rooted Reclaimers – those of us who choose, against all odds, to build a new covenant with ourselves and the world.

Chapter 9

Survival Plasticity, Caste, and the Privilege of Plasticity

SURVIVAL PLASTICITY IS THE natural, evolutionary response to persistent environmental threats. It's the body's and mind's desperate attempt to maximize survival probability when subjected to chronic stress, danger, or deprivation. Unlike privilege plasticity, which assumes a baseline of safety that allows exploration, experimentation, and recovery from mistakes, survival plasticity is shaped by a calculus of scarcity. Limited margin for error, limited margin for trust, and often no margin for healthy expansion.

In societies stratified by systemic oppression, whether through race, class, gender, or other axes of marginalization, survival plasticity becomes an inherited reality. It encodes not only in individual nervous systems but across generations, saturating the very architecture of cognition, emotion, and cultural expression. It recalibrates what is perceived as possible, what risks are deemed acceptable, and what dreams are permitted to survive beyond the imagination stage. This is the lived, daily reality for billions of people worldwide.

Here's the simple version.

Privilege means that you can take chances, mess up, and still be okay. Survival means that taking the very same chance can cost you everything if you mess up. If you have been simply surviving, your mind and body treat any mistakes like real danger. It's hard to thrive under those conditions.

If you:

- Panic at small mistakes
- Can't take feedback without spiraling
- Feel shame as a first emotion when making a mistake

Exercise (One tiny experiment):

Make a mistake on purpose – a small safe mistake. Send a text with a typo, leave a dish unwashed, be a minute or two late to an unimportant event. Then say to yourself, "I made a mistake, and the sky didn't fall. I'll be okay."

Definitions That Change Everything

The caste system, whether formally codified as in historical India or informally enforced as in the United States, functions precisely by weaponizing survival plasticity against targeted populations. Isabelle Wilkerson's book *Caste* explains this concept cogently in the American context. Caste enforces a predictable psychological outcome: those at the lower tiers must adapt to survive, while those at the upper tiers can afford to imagine, to innovate, and to err without catastrophic consequence. Over time, this bifurcation of plastic potential magnifies social, economic, and cognitive disparities until they appear to be innate rather than engineered.

Privilege plasticity is not synonymous with wealth, although wealth can provide one of its clearest foundations. Privilege plasticity is the capacity to experiment, to fail safely, to dream expansively without the immediate threat of annihilation. It's the capacity to trust systems – educational, legal, governmental – to function in your favor or at minimum, neutrally. It's the freedom to define your identity beyond survival needs.

Survival plasticity, in contrast, molds every decision through the lens of existential threat to life or liberty. Where privilege plasticity asks, "What do I want to create?" survival plasticity asks, "What must I do to survive this day, this hour, this minute?" This divergence begins early, often before conscious memory. It shapes educational outcomes, emotional intelligence, incarceration rates, health trajectories, maternal health security, emotional resilience, and creative potential. It's not merely about economic mobility. It's about the very architecture of possibility within a human being's life.

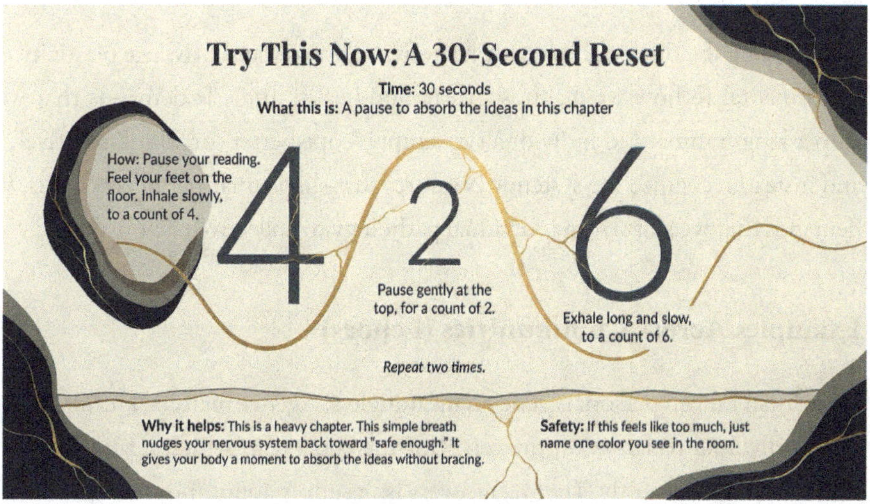

Soil vs. Armor: Why Context Matters

When marginalized communities are subjected to chronic systemic violence through redlining, educational apartheid, healthcare disparities, environmental racism, and daily microaggressions, their adaptive strategies are often pathologized by the dominant culture. The high-alert nervous system is misdiagnosed as an anxiety disorder. The mistrust of institutions is labeled as paranoia. The need to secure basic resources before pursuing higher goals is dismissed as laziness or shortsightedness. The very survival strategies demanded by oppression are then used to justify further oppression by activating stereotypical tropes. It's a vicious cycle with devastating human and societal costs.

Survival plasticity doesn't occur in isolation. Its effects ripple outward, impacting not only the survivor but those in their orbit: partners, children, colleagues, communities. The hypervigilance, emotional numbing, and adaptive suppression necessary for survival often create relational fractures, emotional absences, and behavioral volatility that reverberate both inter-relationally and across generations. Survival secures the individual at a profound cost to intimacy, spontaneity, and trust. Recognizing the collateral damage of survival plasticity is crucial if we are to fully understand trauma not as a private pathology, but as a communal inheritance.

Recognizing the distinction between survival plasticity and privilege plasticity is fundamental to how we diagnose, treat, and heal trauma. It demands that we stop asking traumatized individuals to simply "cope better" or "think positively" and instead recognize the systemic pressures that shape their nervous systems. It demands that we shift from individual pathology to collective responsibility.

Examples Across Communities (Echoes)

This doesn't mean personal agency is meaningless. Agency matters. Healing matters. Individual reclamation matters. But the context in which healing occurs must be named honestly. Trauma recovery isn't simply about "bouncing back" or "building resilience." For many, it's about constructing entirely new internal and external ecosystems where privilege plasticity can finally take root and flourish.

When we fail to differentiate between survival plasticity and privilege plasticity, we perpetuate the myth of meritocracy. We tell people that if they just work hard enough, think positively enough, or pray fervently enough, they too can achieve boundless success. When, in fact, many are navigating worlds where the trauma buffer is so taxed that basic functioning is an act of heroism.

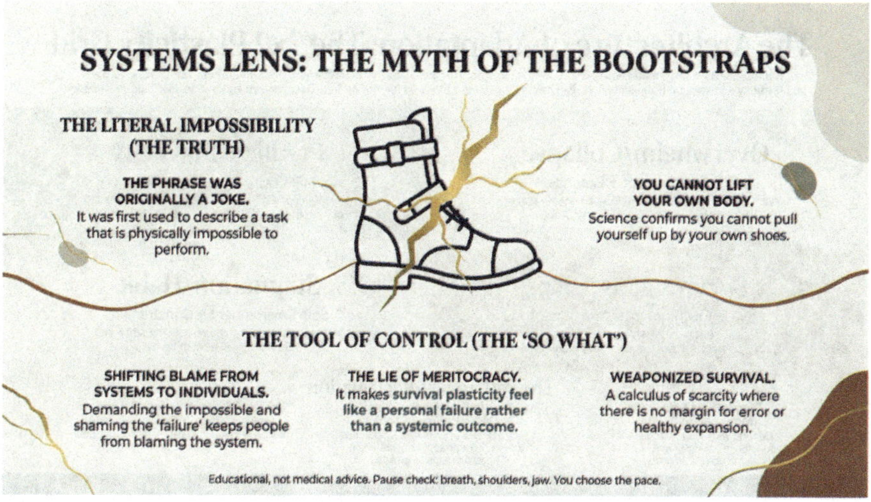

Survival plasticity is exhausting precisely because it never allows true rest. Even in moments of apparent safety, the nervous system remains primed for threat. This has profound physiological consequences, including many of the lifestyle diseases that overburden our current healthcare system. The body continues to bear the cost of survival long after the external danger has passed – if it ever truly passes at all.

Our work is to first build a safe-enough environment (move from Left to Right), and *then* practice moving from constriction to expansion (move from Bottom to Top).

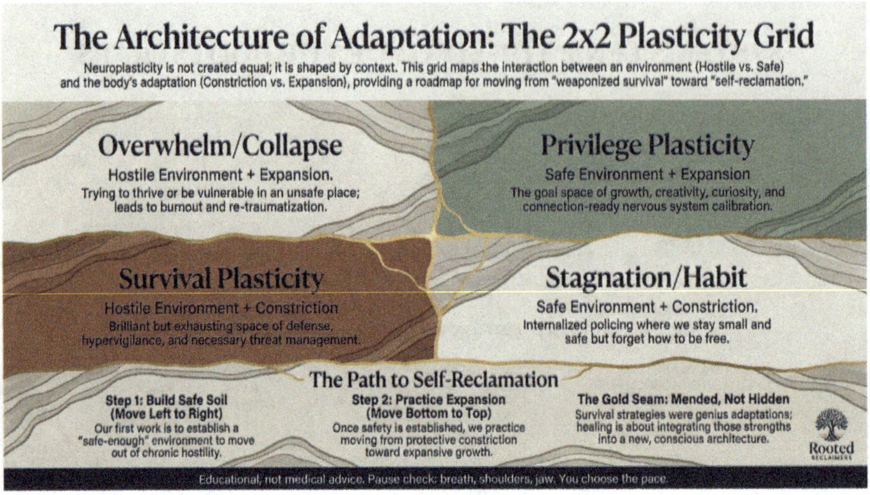

Privilege plasticity, on the other hand, allows the nervous system to cycle through stress and recovery naturally. It permits periods of vulnerability, creativity, and repose without existential risk. It fosters long-term thinking, strategic planning, and visionary leadership. It's the soil from which true flourishing grows.

In the context of weaponized survival, the Rooted Reclaimer's task is twofold. First, to reclaim as much privilege plasticity as possible within the constraints of their environment. This might involve building micro-communities of safety; utilizing community leaders, organizers, and businesses down for the cause; practicing nervous system regulation techniques like breathwork; and cultivating spaces where vulnerability is honored rather than punished. Second, it involves the active dismantling of external systems that enforce survival plasticity at the collective level. This isn't optional. Without systemic change, individual healing will always be partial, always precarious.

Please, register to vote and participate in your local community when you feel called to action.

This book isn't a treatise on victimhood. It's a call to action. It's an invitation to recognize the brilliance and ingenuity of survival plasticity, and then to transcend it where possible. It's a plea to honor the cost of survival without romanticizing it. It's an insistence that privilege plasticity should not be a rarefied experience for the few, but a universal human right.

The first step is recognizing where survival plasticity still governs our lives. The second step is daring to imagine something different. The third is working, individually and collectively, to make that imagined freedom real.

The next several chapters start to build the conditions where privilege plasticity can thrive.

Chapter 10

The Soil of Safety

THE SOIL OF SAFETY isn't merely the absence of danger. It's the presence of conditions that allow plasticity to serve not just survival, but growth. Safety is both internal and external. It's structural, relational, and biological. It's cultivated over time through consistency, predictability, affirmation, and empowerment. Without fertile soil, no tree, no matter how determined, can reach its full height. Without the nourishment of safety, no human being can truly reclaim their wholeness.

In my clinical and philosophical work with trauma survivors, one pattern emerges consistently: recovery is impossible if the soil of safety remains barren. The best strategies, the most sophisticated cognitive tools, the strongest willpower, all collapse under conditions where safety is sporadic, conditional, or perceived as temporary. Nervous systems do not heal under duress. They survive.

> **If healing feels hard, maybe you're still in duress.**
> That doesn't mean you're failing. It means your system is doing its job. Healing needs room. If you don't have much room, we start smaller. That's not lowering the bar. That's being smart.

Yet for those raised in survival plasticity, trust itself is a luxury. If the world has demonstrated itself to be unsafe through violence, betrayal, discrimination, or neglect, then trusting it to be otherwise isn't just naïve, it can be dangerous, as Baldwin told us earlier. The body keeps score, as Bessel van der Kolk reminds us. This phrase, drawn from van der Kolk's research, refers to the way traumatic experiences are stored and expressed in the body, even when they aren't fully processed in the mind. But beyond keeping score, the body also builds blueprints of what is possible, and what is probable. Safety must be taught, but before it can be taught, it must be experienced.

This is where the metaphor of soil becomes critical. Safety isn't a switch that flips. It's an ecosystem. It requires preparation, tending, and protection. The soil must be cleared of toxins – the gaslighting, the invalidation, the chronic instability – that have poisoned previous attempts at growth. It must be aerated by genuine human connection: people who see us, hear us, hold space for us without demand or distortion. It must be nourished with practices that honor the full complexity of the human spirit, not just its productivity. Thich Nhat Hanh once said, "When you plant lettuce, if it does not grow well, you don't blame the lettuce. You look for reasons it is not doing well. It may need fertilizer, or more water, or less sun. You never blame the lettuce."

For many trauma survivors, their first experience of even marginal safety doesn't come until adulthood, if at all. And even then, safety is often partial – seen in a relationship that feels secure but still conditional, a workspace that is affirming until economic forces demand otherwise, or a therapist who understands, but only within the constraints of a 50-minute hour. Real safety is rare. Recognizing this hopefully breeds clarity and not cynicism. Healing requires recognizing the soil you are planted in. It requires ruthlessly evaluating what truly nourishes and what merely distracts or numbs.

In the absence of external safety, many survivors begin by cultivating internal safety. This isn't an abdication of the need for systemic change. It's a pragmatic survival strategy. "If I cannot trust the outer world yet, I can at least begin building an inner sanctuary where my nervous system can exhale, even if only briefly." Practices like breathwork, mindful movement, trauma-informed nutrition (see the work of Julie Feldman and Tracy Brown), and carefully chosen social connection become not luxuries, but necessities. They aren't "self-care" in the pop-psychology sense. They're acts of strategic resistance against a world that would otherwise keep survival plasticity locked in as a permanent state.

The soil of safety, once established, doesn't simply support healing. It accelerates evolution. When the body no longer needs to prepare for constant attack, it reallocates its immense energy reserves to creativity, learning, intimacy, and exploration. Neuroplasticity itself operates optimally in safety. Without it, we repeat patterns. With it, we can reprogram entire systems of thought, emotion, and behavior.

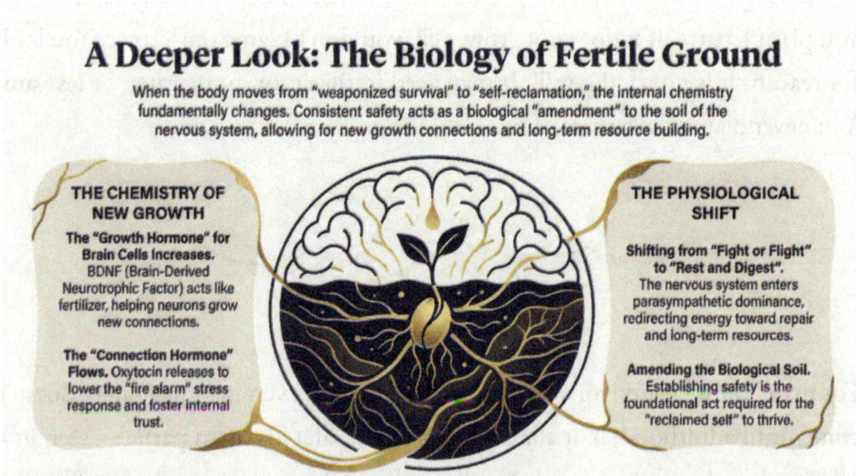

A Deeper Look: The Biology of Fertile Ground

When we finally experience safety – consistent, reliable safety – our brain chemistry begins to change, like barren soil receiving water and nutrients for the first time.

- **The "Growth Hormone" for Brain Cells Increases:** Stress shrinks parts of the brain needed for learning and memory. Safety allows the brain to produce more BDNF (Brain-Derived Neurotrophic Factor), which is like fertilizer for brain cells. It helps neurons grow new connections, making it easier to learn new ways of being and break old survival patterns. The soil becomes richer, able to support new roots.

- **The "Connection Hormone" Flows:** Safety, especially safe connection with others, releases oxytocin. This hormone lowers the "fire alarm" stress response (the HPA axis). It acts like adding beneficial microbes to the soil, helping create a calm, stable internal environment where trust can begin to grow.

- **The Body Shifts from "Fight or Flight" to "Rest and Digest":** Safety allows the nervous system to shift into parasympathetic ("rest and digest") dominance. This is like the plant finally getting enough sunlight and water to relax and open its leaves. Energy goes toward repair, digestion, and building long-term resources instead of just surviving the next threat.

This is why establishing safety isn't just a nice idea; it's the biological foundation for change. You cannot grow strong roots in toxic soil. Creating safety *is* the act of amending the soil, making it possible for the seeds of the "new you" – the reclaimed you – to finally sprout and thrive.

Source Note: *Research confirms that supportive social environments and experiences of safety promote positive neuroplasticity. Factors like oxytocin release and increased BDNF are linked to reduced stress responses and enhanced brain health, enabling learning and adaptation.*[1]

This is why spaces of psychological safety are revolutionary. They create the preconditions for growth that oppression seeks to eliminate. They don't coddle or deny hardship. It's not an accident that historically oppressed communities, when given access to true safety, whether through collective organizing, sanctuary movements, or diasporic artistic communities, produce surges of creativity,

1. Source: Davidson RJ, McEwen BS. Social influences on neuroplasticity: stress and interventions to promote well-being. Nat Neurosci. 2012;15(5):689-695. PMID: 22504346 / PMCID: PMC3491815

innovation, and resilience that have the capacity to reshape societies. Safety isn't an indulgence. It's a catalyst.

Environmental, Relational, and Interoceptive Cues

The soil of safety isn't built alone. This is where connection returns to the foreground. We don't create safety purely through introspection or private rituals. We create it through the painstaking, often messy work of human relationship. Trusting wisely. Setting boundaries fiercely. Repairing when possible. Departing when necessary. Finding the rare spaces, the people, the communities, the environments, where the nervous system is not under siege.

For *Rooted Reclaimers*, the task is clear: Identify where your soil is barren and begin the slow work of re-tilling. Withdraw from spaces that poison the root system. Invest heavily, sometimes radically, in cultivating environments, relationships, and practices that restore. Safety is a dynamic process, not a static condition. It must be tended daily, like any living system.

Part of this tending involves recognizing the signs of safety within the body: the absence of hypervigilance, the presence of playfulness, the softening of breath, and the return of curiosity. These aren't trivial phenomena. They're markers of neurological regeneration and signals that the system is moving from survival to growth.

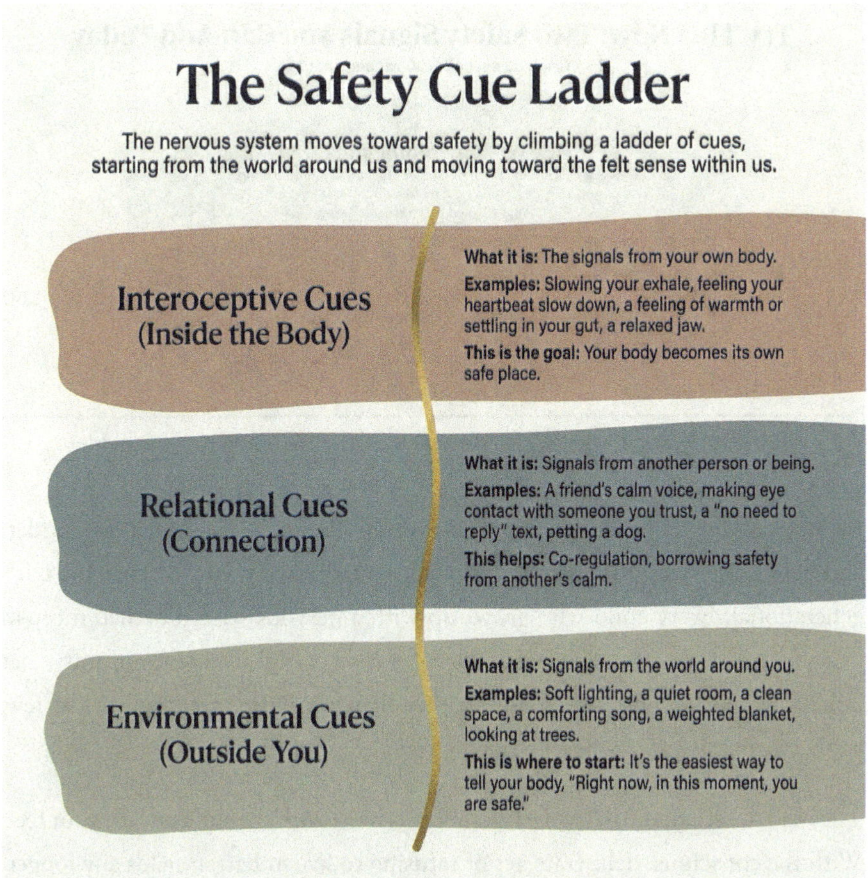

We start at the bottom and work our way up. Adding more environmental cues makes it easier to feel relational safety, which in turn makes it easier to feel safe inside our own skin.

Safety doesn't guarantee the absence of future pain. Nothing can. But safety creates the resilience to meet that pain differently. Instead of coming from a place of collapse, it comes from a place of rooted strength. It's the difference between being knocked over by every storm, having one bad interaction and the whole day being ruined, and learning how to bend without breaking.

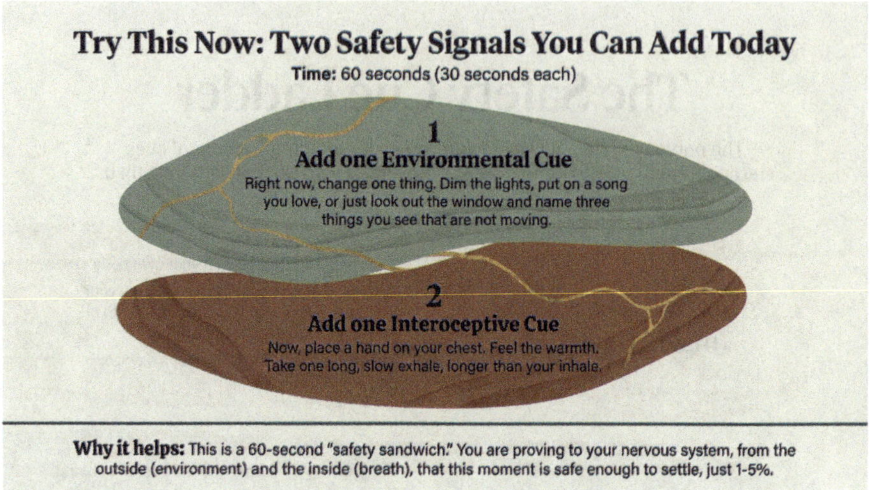

Rooted reclaimers must be gardeners of their own soil: vigilant, wise, tender, and fierce. Knowing that the work they do in cultivating safety isn't selfish. It's generational. Every child who grows up with a nervous system bathed more in trust than terror carries the possibility of a new world. Every community that holds safety as its most sacred duty, rather than a privilege reserved for the few, pushes humanity a step closer to its highest potential.

The road to reclamation is long, but it begins here: with the soil beneath your feet. With the conscious, deliberate act of refusing to live in barren fields any longer. With the radical insistence that you are worthy of the ecosystems that allow not just survival, but full bloom.

Chapter 11

Small Moves, Sacred Ground

HEALING ISN'T A STRAIGHT line. It's not a linear climb or a progressive shedding of layers that never return. Healing, real, embodied reclamation, is a cyclical process marked by small moves that accumulate over time into something seismic. It's incremental. Painstaking. And demands an almost unreasonable faith that small moves matter, that sacred ground can be reclaimed one blade of grass, one square inch at a time.

Survivors of trauma may be conditioned to believe that if transformation doesn't come with a thunderclap, it isn't real. We're taught, implicitly and explicitly through social media and entertainment, that survival must be spectacular to be valuable. That a comeback story must be cinematic to be legitimate. But that's a lie told by a society that worships drama because it can't sit quietly with truth.

The truth is simpler. The truth is that small moves save lives. Small moves build the musculature of resilience that allows for eventual radical change. Small moves – a boundary held, a moment of rest chosen over self-flagellation, a need named without apology – are special. They're the seeds from which rooted reclamation grows.

Minimum Effective Dose (MED) for Healing

In the early stages of recovery, those moves can feel laughably small. Getting out of bed. Drinking water. Saying no. Breathing into a tight place in the body without flinching away. To the untrained eye, these acts may seem trivial. But they aren't trivial to a nervous system trained to anticipate threats at every corner. They're acts of rebellion against the code of hypervigilance that survival plasticity has etched into the flesh.

In healthcare we call this the Minimum Effective Dose, or MED. In the simplest terms, MED is the smallest action you can take to influence your health toward wellness. It's the tiniest step that effects change toward the positive. Sometimes, that action might even be *in*action – choosing *not* to react, *not* to push through. It's about finding just enough to tell your body things are changing, without overwhelming it. Think of it like switching from regular coke to diet coke in an effort to improve blood sugar. It's not the whole solution, but it's *one* small move in the right direction. One slow exhale instead of forcing ten minutes of meditation when your body is screaming "no." That one exhale *is* the MED. It's enough.

Habit Loops That Don't Overwhelm

Small moves are acts of reclaiming ownership over one's physical body, energy, time, and breath. They are how we begin to redirect the emotional currency that has for too long been spent merely trying to survive. Building new habits when you're already running on empty requires a different approach. Many survivors use deeply programmed coping mechanisms just to get through the day. Their reward systems might be distorted by years of survival mode. This does not mean they are broken. It means self-exploration is needed to find what core motivations truly move them toward change.

Because the trauma buffer may already be compromised, the range for new things might be smaller. This demands smaller, more concrete steps. It requires extra self-grace and patience. We start differently. Instead of focusing on the hard part, we sometimes start with the *reward* – the feeling of relief, however small. We focus on the cue (what triggers the old pattern) and the reward (what tiny bit of ease we want instead). Then, we make the action tiny. And then, do it again, and again, until it becomes the baseline reaction to that stimulus.

For instance: Driving down the road, someone honks aggressively (the cue). Instead of tensing up or yelling back (old pattern), briefly turn up the music if you can (tiny action). Focus on naming three instruments you hear. The reward is not just distraction; it's a deeper appreciation of the music, a small moment of beauty claimed back from the fight-or-flight response. You are still moving forward even if the wind knocks you back sometimes. The very fact that you start this path puts a crack in the cycle of burnout and overwhelm. Celebrate being on the journey, not just the outcome of this leg.

Spiral, Not Ladder: Expect Repeats

Without the accumulation of small moves, larger shifts are unsustainable. If you cannot first find safety in a single breath, you cannot build safety into a full life. This isn't a romanticized call to "trust the process." It's an observed reality. The nervous system does not leap from trauma to triumph. It recalibrates slowly, cautiously, suspiciously.

Healing is not climbing straight up a ladder. It's more like hiking a mountain on a lightly worn path that circles back on itself several times on the way to the top. Each time you revisit a familiar place – an old fear, a familiar pattern – you arrive with more wisdom. That wisdom informs the next leg of the journey. It's not failure to revisit something; it's just the path.

Sometimes, the body might resist the new path. It might feel a pull toward the old way, even if it was perilous. This is sometimes called a "healing crisis." These moments can feel like setbacks, but they are often short-lived. They often come right before a breakthrough. The body is just figuring out how to integrate the new configuration. These are not failures or backslides. They are necessary adjustments. Be kind to yourself on the spiral. You are learning new skills and reprogramming your brain and body.

Measuring "Enough" (Subjective + Tiny Metrics)

Every small move is an offering to the part of you that no longer believes full healing is possible. It's a way of building evidence, brick by brick, that safety can exist, that growth can occur, that freedom is not an impossible dream but a daily practice. Survivors must resist the internalized demand for spectacle in the age of overexposure, and the demand to announce healing with fireworks, to prove to themselves and others that the work is paying off.

Often, the most profound shifts are invisible to anyone outside your own skin. They are tectonic plates moving beneath the surface. The days you did not collapse. The moments you felt sadness without it eroding your entire afternoon. The arguments you did not escalate because your nervous system had enough reserve to pause, breathe, and choose differently.

How do we measure progress? Not by checklists alone. We measure by feel. In my clinical practice, I say: Incremental changes lead to incredible results. "Enough" is purely subjective. When first starting the journey, simply *observing* your thoughts without judgment can be enough for that day. "Enough" means you experienced just enough change that it did not deplete you further. It's the subjective MED.

We measure using tiny metrics. Did I unclench my jaw once today? Did I take one full breath when I felt overwhelmed? Did I notice my shoulders were tight and intentionally drop them, even for a second? That graphic artist sitting at her desk, asking herself if she dropped her shoulders recently, and doing that single action reduced tension. That counts. That is enough for that moment.

Case: Micro-Movement Before the Meeting

Imagine Terry, a 40-year-old manager whose body tightens before every work meeting. Their shoulders creep up. Their jaw tightens. Their breath gets shallow just thinking about it. Instead of trying to force themselves to be "calm" (which often backfires), they try a small move.

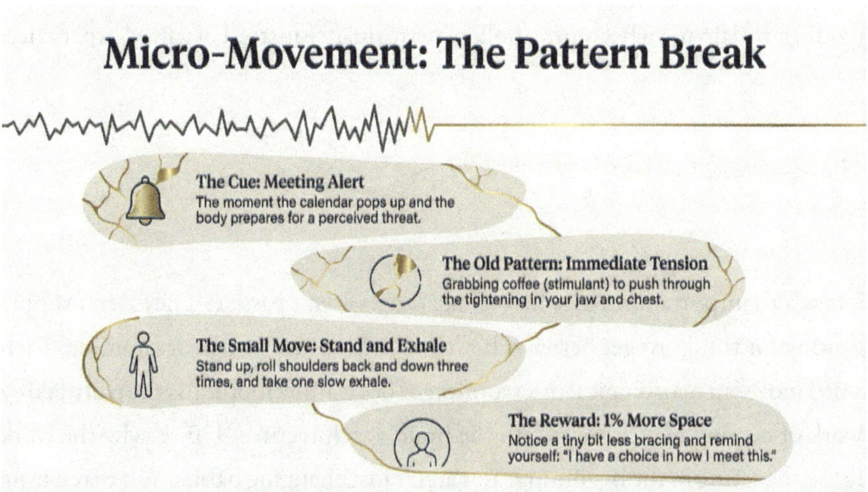

This doesn't "fix" the stress of the meeting. But it interrupts the automatic bracing pattern. It offers the nervous system a different option. Over time, repeated hundreds of times, these micro-movements build capacity. They create sacred ground within the body, inch by painstaking inch.

Sacred ground is built not by declarations, but by consistent tending. Every small move that honors your body, your boundaries, your humanity, is a seed planted. Some seeds germinate quickly; others lie dormant for seasons before bursting forth. There's no shame in the pace of your own growth. Shame itself is a toxin in the soil of safety. It must be identified and extracted wherever possible.

I've often reflected on my own path of reclamation and seen how my biggest shifts were never the product of a single revelation. They were the result of hundreds of smaller recalibrations, decisions made in quiet moments where no one was watching. Choosing connection over isolation when the old pattern was to withdraw. Choosing movement when the old impulse was to shut down. Choosing nourishment when the old craving was for numbing. Choosing to feel, really feel, when every cell in my body was screaming to dissociate.

These are the harrowing battles no one applauds because no one sees them. But they're real. They're the foundation of everything that follows. Without honoring the small moves – ones that create structural support – the larger ones collapse under their own weight. Without the reclaimed soil cultivated through daily tending, reclamation becomes a hollow performance instead of a lived experience.

There's an important nuance here: small moves aren't passive. They aren't simply waiting for things to get better. They're deliberate acts of reprogramming. Each small move is a neurological interruption of old trauma loops. It's the painstaking work of carving new grooves into the brain's architecture. This is why the work feels exhausting in the beginning. You aren't just changing habits. You're rewiring the entire electrical system of the self.

This understanding should bring compassion to the process, not discouragement. If you feel tired, it means you're doing real work. If you feel overwhelmed at times, it means you're stretching beyond your old survival patterns. If you feel like you're taking one step forward and two steps back, it means you're human. Healing isn't linear because growth isn't linear. It spirals, it eddies, it doubles back to reinforce its foundation.

To those walking the journey, I say this: Honor your small moves with the reverence they deserve. Document them when you can. Witness them in yourself the way you might tenderly watch a small child take their first steps. Each act of self-respect, each moment of choosing differently, is a banner planted on sacred ground reclaimed from the wastelands of trauma.

As **Rooted Reclaimers**, we must understand that the transformation we seek doesn't begin with grand gestures. It begins with the daily refusal to betray ourselves. It begins with the quiet insistence that we're worth the effort. It begins with the radical, sacred commitment to cultivate a life that doesn't merely avoid pain but actively nourishes possibility.

Small moves matter. Sacred ground awaits. Keep moving. Keep tending. Keep reclaiming, even when only *you* know the magnitude of the work you're doing.

You aren't just surviving anymore. You're rebuilding a home within yourself where no one else ever gets to evict you again.

Small moves aren't a waste of time

We learn new habits by making small changes and consistently doing them until the behaviour becomes second nature. It's how the body and mind learn when it's safe to expand, grow, and thrive.

If you:

• Think small steps don't count

• Quit because you can't do it all perfectly

• Start big but have a tendency to crash shortly after starting

Exercise (One tiny experiment):

Do one of the exercises from this book, but do the simplest or smallest version of it. Take one full breath. One full stretch. One full glass of water. And then say out loud to yourself, "That counted."

Chapter 12

Remembering How to Dream

One of the most insidious casualties of trauma isn't simply the loss of safety. It's the erosion of the ability to dream. Not the fleeting images conjured during sleep, but the capacity to imagine futures beyond the immediate necessities of survival. Dreaming requires spaciousness. It requires latitude of imagination incompatible with a nervous system trapped in high-alert vigilance.

Imagination as Regulation

In the landscape of survival plasticity, dreaming often becomes a luxury few can afford. Dreams require emotional and cognitive energy beyond the immediate demands of staying alive. When every ounce of bandwidth is devoted to scanning for threats, neutralizing danger, mitigating risk, there's little left to invest in the abstract architecture of hope.

For many survivors, there's a long period – years, sometimes decades – where dreaming is either abandoned or distorted. Dreams become purely utilitarian: escape plans, contingency strategies, fallback positions. They aren't dreams so much as survival projections. What can I build that will protect me? What status can I achieve that will inoculate me from future harm? What external markers of success can shield me from internal collapse?

This distortion of dreaming is a trauma response, not a moral failure. When the soil of safety is depleted, what grows is pragmatism, not possibility. Imagination contracts to the size of a clenched fist. Hope is measured out in rationed doses, small enough to be withdrawn without catastrophic heartbreak if the world once again proves itself hostile.

> **In plain words:**
> If you can't dream, it doesn't mean you're broken. It means your body learned to focus on today, not tomorrow.

In my own journey, I can trace the arc of this contraction and its eventual loosening. There was a long stretch when every goal I set was built on a defensive architecture: achieve more, control more, protect more. There was no dreaming for joy, only for fortification. Success itself became a survival tactic. The act of building something – a career, a reputation, a body of work – was armor against collapse.

It took significant work, years of incremental healing and deliberate cultivation of safety, to remember how to dream without survival at center. It took planting small seeds of possibility in spaces previously abandoned as barren. It took reclaiming emotional currency from fear and reinvesting it into hope. It took risking disappointment, risking exposure, risking failure – all things survival adaptations train you to avoid at all costs.

One of the hardest things for a survivor to do is to imagine a life not predicated on defense. To envision relationships, careers, communities through the lens of potential flourishing, not potential threat. To hold a dream in the mind without simultaneously calculating all the ways it might be shattered. This isn't a light task. It's an advanced form of survival that transcends the old survival codes and begins rewriting the very operating system of the self.

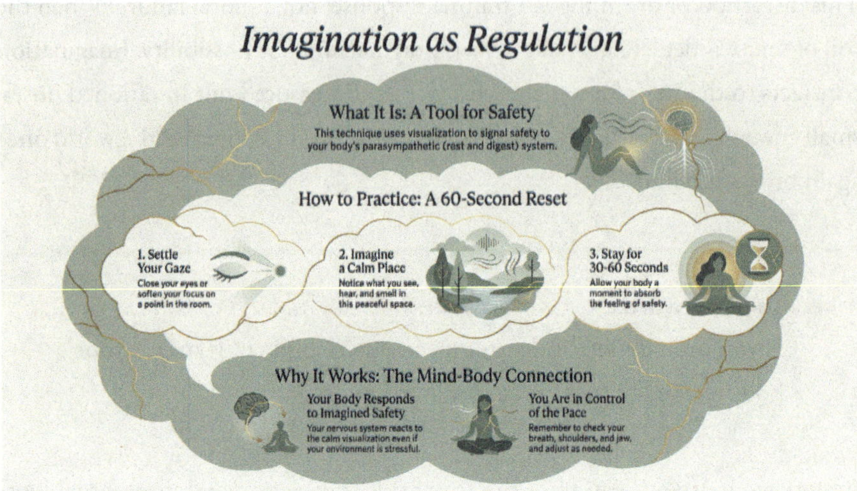

Play, Pleasure, and Future-Self Rehearsal

For many of us in the beginning stages of rooted reclamation, the early dreams are modest. They may not look like dreams at all to the outside observer. A desire to sleep through the night without hypervigilance. A wish to laugh without self-consciousness. A hope to trust someone without preparing for betrayal. These are foundational reconnections to parts of ourselves that were forced into exile.

Over time, with deliberate practice, the capacity for dreaming expands. Bigger visions can be entertained without triggering immediate shutdown. The imagination muscles strengthen. Possibility begins to feel less like a dangerous mirage and more like a navigable frontier. You begin to plan not just for contingencies but for creations. Not just for survival but for contribution.

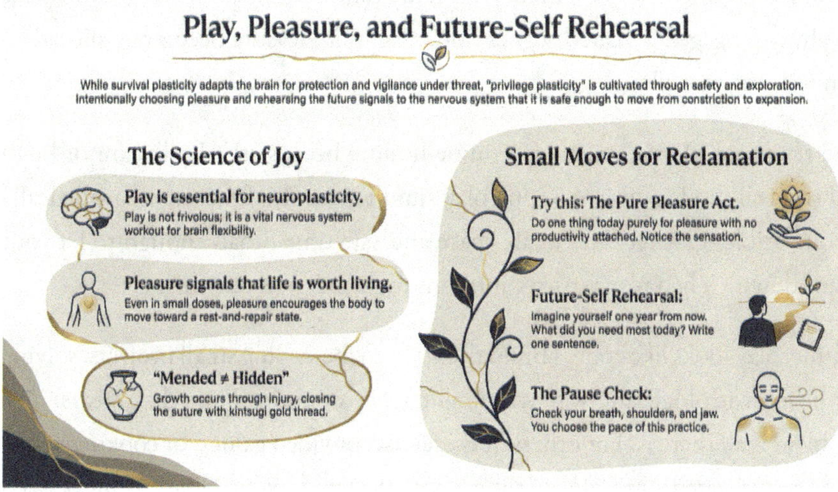

Dreaming becomes an act of defiance against the trauma that said you had no future. Dreaming becomes a political act in a world that profits from your disempowerment. Dreaming becomes an act of self-reclamation, proof that trauma may have scarred the body and mind, but didn't extinguish the soul's capacity to reach toward the light.

There's a particular grief that comes with remembering how to dream. A mourning for the years lost to contraction. A sadness for the dreams that couldn't be born in the arid soil of survival. It's critical to name this grief, to honor it, but not to live there. Grieving lost dreams is part of the fertilization of new ones. It's the recognition that though you were denied certain seasons of growth, the seasons ahead are still fertile with possibility.

What Play Actually Is

Play is not leisure. Leisure is passive. Play is active engagement with something for the pure reason that it spikes dopamine, drops cortisol, and quiets the amygdala's constant alert. Play is the state in which time disappears because the activity itself is reward enough.

For trauma survivors, play is one of the first casualties. When survival is the operating system, the nervous system deprioritizes anything that does not serve threat management. Joy is a luxury the body cannot budget for when the shields are always engaged. Creativity goes underground. Pleasure becomes guilt-laden. Fun feels irresponsible.

The return of play is a sign of genuine healing because the body cannot be in full survival mode and in genuine play simultaneously. They are neurologically incompatible. Play requires a safe space and safe time broad enough to let your guard down. When play returns, it means the window is opening.

For me, play looks like code. I build things like vibe-coding small projects, solving problems with logic the way you might solve a puzzle. Time disappears. The problem is all there is. For others, it is exercise, or video games, or cooking something complicated, or singing in the car with the windows up. The specific activity matters less than the quality of absorption and the disappearance of the inner critic, the disengaging of the scanner, and the return of pure joy – even if fleeting at first.

Find your version. Protect it from productivity. Do not let it become a task.

Dreaming as a Collective Act

My grandfathers were physicians. My great-grandfather before him was a physician at a time when it was virtually unheard of. I was raised inside a lineage that understood medicine not as a career but as a covenant, the highest form of service, and the deepest commitment to the wellbeing of those around you.

I never stopped dreaming of following that lineage. Even in the most contracted years, the most survival-oriented seasons of my life, the dream of being of service held. My plans had backup plans. My goals had contingencies. The survival brain kept imagining pathways forward even when forward felt closed.

What I understand now is that the dream was never just mine. It was planted in me by people who had paid forward a legacy that they now needed me to carry. That understanding changes the nature of dreaming. It's no longer a solo journey; it's following a thread woven into a much longer story.

Safe spaces for dreaming, the kind where you can say the large and fragile thing without someone immediately cutting it down to practical size, are among the rarest and most valuable resources available to a healing community. Dreaming collectively means becoming a witness for other people's large visions. It means creating the culture where someone can say, "I want to build a clinic in my neighborhood" or, "I want to write a book" or "I want to stop working for someone else" and be met with curiosity rather than skepticism. It means being what others were not for you.

Community Dreams (Dream Keepers & Witnesses)

For the **Rooted Reclaimers** walking this path, the act of dreaming must be cultivated with intention. Dreaming must be seen as a legitimate tool of liberation, not as frivolous or naive. The ability to imagine better futures for our communities, our descendants, and the world at large is a muscle that must be exercised and protected.

Dreaming requires communal spaces that honor vulnerability. It requires spaces moderated by mentors, elders, peers who can model what it means to build without apology. It requires a culture that celebrates not just resilience but thriving. In environments where survival is the highest aspiration, dreaming is a radical act. In environments where freedom is normalized, dreaming is the natural order.

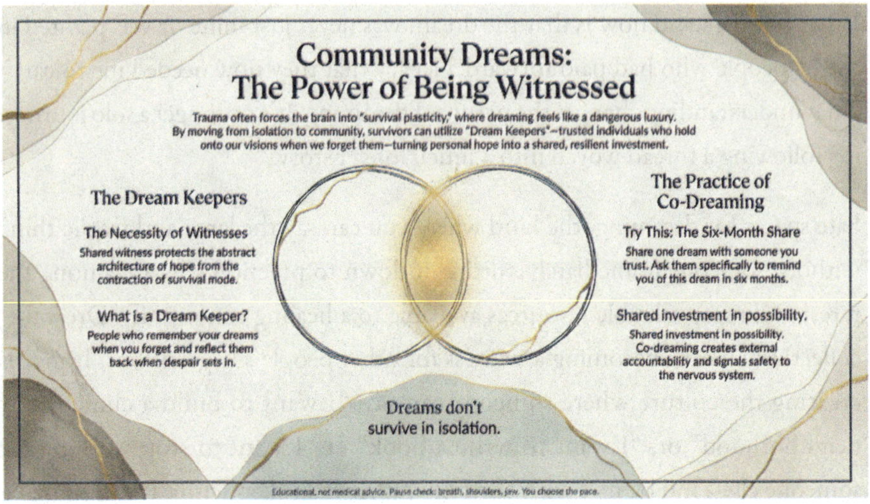

Part of our collective work must be to create and sustain these environments. To build gardens in the ruins. To build classrooms where curiosity is valued over conformity. To build workplaces where collaboration is valued over competition. To build relationships where authenticity is valued over performance.

When dreaming is culturally supported, it becomes less an individual burden and more a shared birthright. The collective imagination lifts individual efforts into new realms of possibility. Healing becomes less isolated and more contagious. Dreams multiply and interweave, forming ecosystems of reclamation that no single trauma can destroy.

I don't claim that dreaming is easy. It's not. It requires risk. It requires repeated willingness to confront the possibility of disappointment. It requires courage to envision what has never been offered to you. I'm living proof, as are so many others walking this journey, that dreaming is possible even after profound betrayal. That dreaming is a skill that can be remembered, strengthened, and passed on.

It must be passed on. If we are to create a world where survival isn't the highest human aspiration, we must teach future generations how to dream before they're taught to brace for impact. We must embed in our children and communities the knowledge that imagination isn't a liability. It's a lifeline. It's not a distraction from survival. It's the blueprint for a life beyond mere endurance.

Remembering how to dream isn't the end of the healing journey. It's a midpoint, a critical threshold where survival begins to give way to creation. It's the moment where the road on this journey widens and the horizon stretches farther than fear can reach.

We must keep walking. We must keep dreaming. Not because it's easy. But because it's necessary.

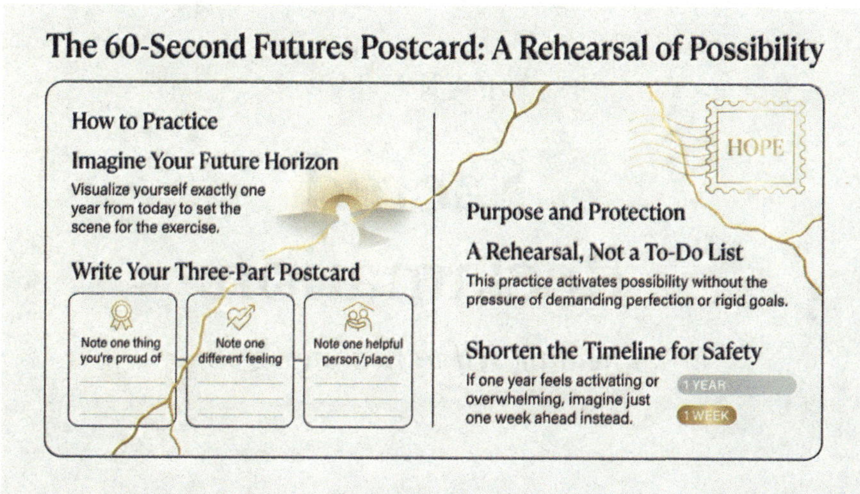

PART IV

Sacred Reclamation

From healing self to healing together.

Chapter 13

Rebuilding the Home Within

Survival demands dissociation. In the face of overwhelming threat, trauma survivors often abandon parts of themselves by necessity. Those parts of the injured soul – emotions, intuition, trust, imagination, even basic bodily sensations – are walled off to protect the core self from intolerable pain, loss, or injury. Over time, this internal fragmentation becomes the new normal. The survivor moves through life partially present, partially armored, always braced for betrayal or disaster.

Healing demands a return, but not to some former self untouched by pain. That self never fully existed. Rather, it's the slow, deliberate construction of a home within the body, mind, and spirit where full presence becomes possible again.

This rebuilding isn't a restoration project. It's a new creation, formed with the understanding that the old structures weren't merely damaged by trauma, but often unsafe or insufficient from the start. Survivors aren't returning to innocence. They're building informed sanctuaries, grounded in reality and shaped by discernment.

The first task in this reconstruction is to establish stability. This means creating conditions in which the body feels, as often as possible, that vigilance isn't required for survival. Stability doesn't mean the absence of external stress. Such absence may never be fully achievable. It means the presence of reliable internal signals, clear boundaries, emotional literacy, and somatic awareness that allow the survivor to move through life without perpetual fear.

Stability requires recognizing and tending to the body's basic needs: rest, nourishment, movement, regulation of stress. It also demands creating relationships that reinforce safety rather than erode it. Proximity to people, spaces, and practices that uphold dignity becomes non-negotiable. This is the foundation of sustainability.

Once stability is present, the next phase is integration. Trauma fragments. Healing integrates. This doesn't mean erasing the past or collapsing all aspects of the self into a tidy whole. It means cultivating enough internal coherence that the survivor can move through the world with a sense of continuity rather than chronic conflict.

Integration often involves welcoming back parts of the self that were exiled during survival: the playful self, the creative self, the vulnerable self, the assertive self. It means recognizing that anger, sadness, longing, and tenderness aren't liabilities but necessary expressions of full humanity. Integration creates room for these parts to coexist, not in chaos or shame, but within a container of compassionate leadership by the conscious self.

The final stage of rebuilding the home within is *agency*. This is the moment when the survivor stops defining themselves primarily by what happened to them and begins living in active relationship with what they're choosing to build. Agency isn't control over external circumstances. It's authorship over internal responses, values, and direction.

In practice, agency shows up as a stable sense of self that isn't easily shaken by the opinions, demands, or manipulations of others. It manifests in the ability to set and maintain boundaries without apology. It reveals itself in the prioritization of alignment over approval, truth over comfort, dignity over performance.

Rebuilding the home within doesn't eliminate struggle. Pain, loss, and challenge remain part of the human experience. But the survivor who has done this work is no longer wholly reactive to external circumstances. There's an inner anchoring, a sense of place to return to when the world outside becomes unstable.

"Home within" means creating a safe internal space free of self-attack

This means simply that as we challenge the systems that have kept us safe and helped us survive, we require a great deal of self-grace while dismantling these systems.

If you:

- Feel your inner voice is mean
- Feel like you're always doing it wrong
- Feel unsafe in your own body

Exercise (One tiny experiment):

When you notice cruel self-talk, tell yourself, "I'm having a tough time right now." Not, "I suck," or "I can't do anything right."

This work is slow, iterative, and often invisible to others. But over time, it transforms the infrastructure of the self. What was once a battlefield becomes a sanctuary. What was once a site of betrayal becomes a place of repair. What was once defined by fragmentation becomes a foundation for belonging, first to oneself, and then, when readiness allows, to a wider community engaged in the same sacred labor.

At this stage, survivors begin to sense that their healing is no longer only for themselves. The reconstruction of the inner home naturally prepares them to extend that stability outward, to contribute to relationships, spaces, and communities that reflect the values they fought so hard to reclaim within.

Without grandiosity and without performance, they begin to carry the authority of those who have survived, healed, and chosen to live on their own terms. They become living proof that survival was never the end goal. Reclamation was. And from reclamation comes a new kind of leadership, not dominance, not control, but presence. The kind of presence that invites others to believe healing is possible, dignity is non-negotiable, and freedom is worth the effort.

The journey home leads first to a body and mind restored to their rightful owner. But it doesn't end there. From this home base, new roads begin to unfold. New possibilities. New responsibilities.

The work done within is in preparation for the larger call, not just to survive, not even just to heal, but to help build the world that once wounded us into something more just, more humane, and more whole.

I built my own healing the same way I now ask you to build yours, with a structure and plan that holds up on normal days, and with choices small enough to be easily repeatable. I didn't start with a big overhaul, primarily because I had neither the energy nor time to stop running long enough to attempt it. I had to start with breath because I realized that I chronically held my breath. Big stressors – hold my breath. Difficult conversation – hold my breath. It got to the point where I had to remember to breathe when doing anything that triggered even the slightest challenge. It was the quickest way to change the tone of my nervous system without needing a recovery hour or day after the encounter.

It started with longer exhales, simple box breathing, and short breathing resets between patients, meetings, and before sleep. That gave me a little more space inside my body. From there, I added gentle movements that restored trust in the machine that got me through times of great intensity. I walked, I did yoga and qigong, I returned to basics, and I used consistency as the win. Nutrition came shortly after as a stabilizer, because I learned the hard way that under-fueling, blood sugar swings, and dehydration make everything so much worse, including pain, fatigue, irritability, and sleep. Then I faced the pillar I resisted most: connection. I practiced letting safe people in, calling old friends just to check in, asking for support without reciprocity, and building community where I could hold and be held emotionally, socially, and spiritually. That is how I got here – by stacking small moves that created real relief.

Healing starts to shift when you stop treating your body like a problem to solve and start treating it like a system that needs constant tending, safety, rhythm, and enough support to change. The four pillars gave me a map back from survival mode, and they do the same for people who feel trapped in symptoms, stuck in burnout, or exhausted by the pressure to "fix it all." You do not need perfect compliance. You need a plan that you can return to without shame. Start where you have access today. Use breath to interrupt the spiral, use movement to reclaim agency, use nutrition to create steadiness, and use connection to stop carrying all of it alone. That is the work that changed my life, and it is the same work that lets your life change in a way that feels earned, grounded, and real.

What Belonging Feels Like

There is a beach in the Bahamas where I stood with my wife, eyes closed, faces warmed in the sun's embrace.

I'm not trying to describe a vacation; I need you to understand what being all the way in my body felt like. I'm not talking about the concept of it, but the sensation. Because the concept is easy. The sensation is what we have been working toward.

The sun on that beach didn't just warm the surface. It saturated us. It moved through our skin and kept going, down through muscle and bone, into the places where I had been holding cold for years, unknown to me. My wife and I were in perfect sync in that moment. I said to myself a simple mantra: **This is where I am. This is who I am with. This is your life.** Staying present even for only moments at a time when it matters can be a great triumph.

In that moment I felt a full sense of what it means to belong. Belonging doesn't have to happen in a group setting. Just one other person acknowledging your humanity and fragility can be greatly affirming and improves trust among community members.

Belonging is active, not passive. It is not simply being allowed into a space. Being allowed in is welcome. Belonging is being invited where your presence adds something and the space adds something to you. Belonging is the mutual-assured construction of safety between two or more people who have collectively decided to stop performing for each other.

It requires radical self-care on both sides. It requires the willingness to be seen without armor, and the discipline to hold someone else's unarmored self with care. It is community work. It is relational work. And it is available to you.

You will not find it everywhere. You may not have found it yet in the places that were supposed to provide it. That is a real loss worth grieving. And it does not mean it doesn't exist.

It exists in the room where someone speaks with integrity. It exists in the relationship where a hard conversation doesn't end the relationship. And it exists in the community that calls you back in when you've gone silent, simply to remind you that your presence matters.

Build toward those rooms. Stay in them when you find them. Become someone whose presence makes them possible.

The Four Pillars in Daily Liturgy

Rebuilding the home within isn't abstract. It's grounded in small, daily actions – a quiet liturgy of self-respect. The Four Pillars of Breath, Movement, Nutrition, and Connection aren't just concepts. They're the practices that form the walls, floor, and roof of this inner sanctuary. Think of them as a simple daily flow.

Morning Anchor (Breath & Nutrition): Start with breath (like the Double-Inhale Sigh) and hydration/protein (like the Morning Steady) to set a stable foundation for the day. Small move: One minute of breath, one glass of water.

Midday Reset (Movement): Use tiny movements (like the Grounded Sway or shoulder rolls) during transitions or breaks to discharge stress before it accumulates. Small move: 60 seconds of movement between tasks.

Afternoon/Evening Nourish (Nutrition & Connection): Ensure the last meal supports blood sugar stability. Reach out with a low-pressure connection (like the "thinking of you" text) or practice self-connection (hand on heart). Small move: One supportive food choice, one moment of connection.

Throughout (Breath as Anchor): Use micro-breaths (one slow exhale) whenever tension rises.

This isn't about perfection. It's about rhythm. It's about weaving these small acts into the fabric of the day, creating a steady pulse of safety and self-tending.

What to Do on Hard Days

Some days, the liturgy feels impossible. Old patterns surge into the present. Your body stiffens with constant tension. Vigilance returns, sometimes amplified. On these days, the goal isn't progress; it's presence and harm reduction.

Sometimes, paradoxically, hard days follow good days. When someone has been trapped in a chronic pain cycle or deep exhaustion, a glimpse of feeling better can be intoxicating. It's a reminder that you're still in there, under the armor. It makes sense to want to push the boundaries, to reach for more life. But healing is about rewiring the brain, building new pathways slowly. The old, entrenched programs, the patterns of bracing, pushing, or collapsing, surface quickly when the body or mind is pushed beyond its current capacity. Feeling good before the system is fully robust again can sometimes lead to overdoing it. Like the person recovering from a back injury who feels better and tries to lift something just a little too heavy, or the fibromyalgia patient who finally has energy and dives into a full day of activity, only to trigger a flare-up.

This isn't a failure. It's data. It's the body revealing the current edge of its capacity, the point where older, default programming takes over. Knowing this allows us to respond with compassion, not judgment. When a flare-up happens, consider these steps.

Lower the Bar Drastically: Forget the full liturgy. Go back to your baseline Minimum Effective Dose (MED). What's the one small move that feels possible? Maybe it's just 60 seconds of deep breathing. Maybe it's resting with a hand on your heart. Maybe it's saying no to something and taking PTO if you have it. That's enough.

Name It Without Blame: Acknowledge the flare-up and the disappointment. "My system is overloaded." "I pushed past my edge." Naming it reduces shame and stops the spiral into self-attack.

External Cues: If internal safety feels gone, focus outward. Use the 5-4-3-2-1 Senses exercise (Chapter 3). Change your environment slightly (light, sound, position). Ground yourself in the present moment.

Safe Connection (If Possible): Reach out to one person who feels safe, even if just to say, "Having a flare-up. I need support." Co-regulation is powerful medicine. If no one feels safe, connect with nature, a pet, or comforting music.

Permission to Rest Fiercely: Flare-ups demand rest. Allow it, even if it feels unproductive or frustrating. Rest is the work on these days. It allows the system to recalibrate and find its footing again.

Hard days, including these flare-ups after feeling better, aren't regressions. They're part of the spiral path of healing. They teach us about our current limits with precision. They're reminders of how far you've come and invitations to practice self-compassion fiercely, especially when the old patterns resurface.

Your Plan: One Pillar, One Cue, One Person

Making this real requires a simple, concrete plan. Not a rigid schedule, but a gentle intention. For the next week, try this plan.

Choose One Pillar: Which of the four pillars feels most accessible right now? Breath? Movement? Nutrition? Connection? Start there.

Identify One Cue: When will you practice your small move? Link it to something you already do. For example: *After I brush my teeth... Before I open email... When I feel my shoulders tighten...*

Name One Person (Optional but helpful): Who can you share your intention with, not for accountability, but for authentic witnessing? Or who represents the feeling of safety you're trying to cultivate? Keep their picture nearby.

This tiny plan – one pillar, one cue, maybe one person – makes the abstract concrete. It anchors the intention in the reality of your day.

Grounding:

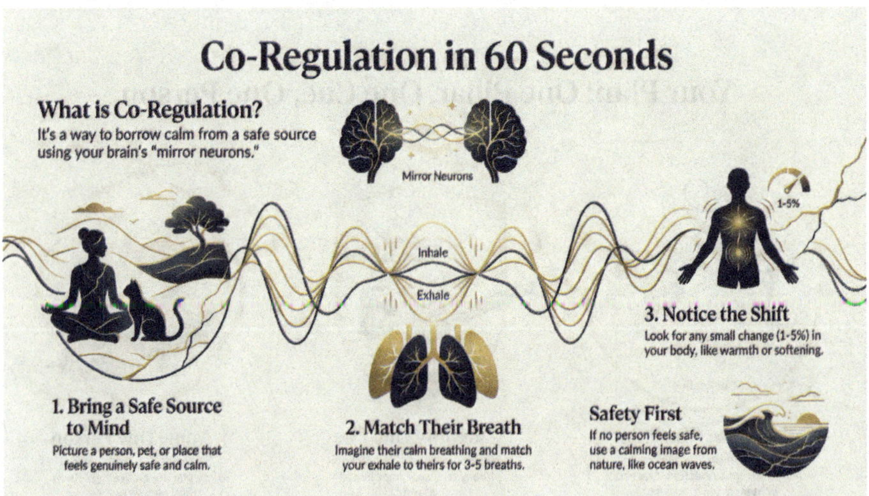

Chapter 14

Rooted Reclaimers and the New Covenant

THOUGH THE LABOR OF reclaiming selfhood must begin internally, it inevitably reaches outward. When survivors rebuild the home within, they do more than repair personal injury. They generate new possibilities for their communities, their descendants, and the systems in which they live.

From this restoration grows a new kind of identity, one not built around victimhood or invincibility, but around conscious engagement with life as it is and life as it could be. Survivors who reach this stage are no longer only managing their trauma. They're no longer merely navigating the ruins. They're reclaiming the power to shape their world with discernment, courage, and purpose.

These individuals aren't defined by what happened to them, but neither do they deny it. They carry their scars with dignity. They know the cost of survival, and they know the price of silence. They have walked through the dismantling of old myths, about hustle, hardness, worthiness, and safety, and emerged carrying a deeper, harder-won truth: that reclamation is possible, and that freedom must be claimed, protected, and honored.

These individuals are what we have called Rooted Reclaimers.

Rooted Reclaimers are not defined by how perfectly they heal or by how loudly they survive. They are defined by their decision to grow deeper into truth, into selfhood, and into community, even when trauma tries to sever those roots. Their work is about letting go of a past that never existed, anchoring into what is real, what is now, and what can withstand the storms still to come.

A Rooted Reclaimer is someone who has made a covenant, first with themselves, then with the world around them.

Covenant Is Just a Promise You Can Actually Keep

The idea of a covenant is to make a deal with yourself while on your journey. It's saying, I don't have to be perfect. I don't have to finish. I don't have to impress anyone. It's a promise shared by all other Rooted Reclaimers trying to find their way back to themselves.

If you:

- Quit because you messed up once
- Feel like you are going to fail no matter what
- Don't trust yourself
- Make big promises that you know you can't keep

Exercise (One tiny experiment):

Make a promise too easy to fail. I will eat two meals for the next seven days. I will practice deep breathing for one minute for the next five days. And if you miss a day, restart without any judgment or shame.

What We Promise Each Other

The covenant is simple but radical: to reclaim their own dignity, to build from it without shame, and to protect the ground of healing for others who are still trying to find their own way home.

This covenant is enacted through daily choices. It's lived in how they care for their own bodies, how they set and defend boundaries, how they build families, communities, and systems that refuse to replicate the harms they survived.

Rooted Reclaimers understand that healing is not a solitary path. They recognize that dignity must be nourished in relationships, and carry forward the understanding that survival is not the goal. Reclamation is. Agency is. Building sacred ground, not just for oneself but for those still struggling to believe it's possible, is part of the responsibility that healing brings.

Boundaries That Protect Belonging

The Rooted Reclaimer doesn't seek to erase the past. They seek to replant what was uprooted. They know that some wounds will never fully close, but that growth is still possible, not in spite of injury, but through it – closing the suture with Kintsugi gold thread. They understand that resilience without rootedness is brittle, and that flourishing requires depth as much as elevation.

The covenant of the Rooted Reclaimer is built on three commitments.

- To remain anchored in the truth of their own humanity, regardless of external validation.
- To cultivate the soil of their lives in ways that support restoration, not exploitation.
- To extend, when possible, the conditions of dignity, safety, and possibility to others.

Practices: Circles, Walks, and Care Teams

This path is not clean, linear, or without setbacks or grief. But it's real. It's powerful. And it's yours.

The journey home leads here, without perfection, without erasure of struggle, but to a way of walking the world rooted, awake, and unshakeable in the quiet knowledge of what has been reclaimed.

This reclamation is both personal and collective. It plants the seeds for new structures, new relationships, and new futures that honor the sacredness and dignity of human life, especially for those who have been most wounded by its violations.

Invitation: Join the Community

You have survived. You have begun to heal. Now you are called to reclaim, fully, consciously, deeply rooted.

You are not merely rebuilding yourself. You are rebuilding sacred ground, for yourself, for those who came before, and for those who will come after.

This is the covenant of the Rooted Reclaimers. This is the work of our time.

Welcome to the Journey.

Final Reflections

The Paradox of the Trauma Hero

TRAUMA HAS A WAY of creating heroes.

Survivors often turn their wounds into fuel, into art, into leadership, into humor, into mastery. The world applauds the visible triumphs without seeing the hidden costs. It hands out trophies for endurance without understanding what it costs a soul to carry that much weight for that long.

Weaponized trauma looks like strength. It feels like invincibility. It becomes the armor we wear so the world can no longer hurt us. But over time, if left unexamined and unhealed, it hollows us out. It isolates us. It builds walls so high and thick around our hearts that even love struggles to break through.

We can succeed outwardly while shrinking inwardly. We can gather accolades while losing intimacy. We can build empires while starving the small, quiet parts of ourselves that simply wanted to feel safe and loved.

We become experts at reading rooms, predicting danger, managing perceptions. We become masters of excellence because it's the only guarantee against abandonment we learned we could trust. We learn to outrun shame, to outwork fear, to outperform grief.

But the faster we run, the further we get from ourselves.

This is the paradox of the trauma hero: the very traits that helped you survive can keep you from fully living. The very talents that brought you success can distance you from yourself. The more you are rewarded by a society that values production over presence, performance over authenticity, the harder it becomes to admit that success does not always equal wholeness.

You learn to keep smiling while something in you slowly calcifies. You learn to keep climbing while your soul quietly begs you to come home.

The tragedy is not the success. The tragedy is the belief that the armor is you. That the mask is your face. That the performance is your worth.

Healing invites a different possibility.

What if you could be extraordinary without staying wounded?
What if your power did not have to be rooted in pain?
What if healing, not hiding, was your true superpower?

You are not just the warrior who fought to survive.

You are also the soul that deserves to rest. The spirit that deserves to sing. The heart that deserves to trust again.

Healing invites you to remember:

You were never only your scars. You were always something more.

You still are.

The Trauma Mastery Arc

From Survival to Sacred Reclamation

If we were to distill the heart of this book into a single conceptual model, it would be this: **trauma mastery isn't about erasure. It's about integration.** It's the gradual, imperfect, courageous work of moving from survival-driven adaptation to authentic, sovereign existence. It's about recognizing the ways trauma has shaped us, without allowing it to define or limit us indefinitely.

The Trauma Mastery Arc has five stages. They are not cleanly sequential. They loop. They regress. They advance unpredictably. The point is not perfect progress, but conscious participation.

Stage 1: Instinctive Survival Adaptations

In the immediate and ongoing aftermath of trauma, whether acute or chronic, the human system adapts. The adaptations are brilliant. They serve to maximize survival within hostile environments. They are neither good nor bad. They simply are.

These adaptations often manifest as:

- People-pleasing as a defense against abandonment.
- Hypervigilance as a defense against betrayal or violence.
- Perfectionism as a defense against humiliation.

- Hustling as a defense against scarcity.
- Withdrawal as a defense against repeated injury.

These adaptations, while life-saving, come at a cost. They require massive expenditures of emotional currency. They distort authentic self-expression. They stunt the development of the nervous system's natural regulation patterns. Over time, they become cages even as they once were shields.

It's critical to honor survival adaptations without romanticizing them. They were essential. They are no longer sufficient for the life the survivor deserves.

Stage 2: Collapse of the Mask

No mask, no matter how sophisticated, can hold indefinitely under the weight of accumulated stressors, aging, systemic injustice, and internal incongruence.

There comes a point when the body, mind, or spirit – usually some combination – rebels. This collapse may look like:

- Burnout.
- Depression.
- Anxiety.
- Rage outbursts.
- Self-sabotaging behavior.
- Illness.
- Existential crises.

This collapse is the body's desperate plea for change. It's the moment when survival strategies no longer cover the original injuries. When the closet is overflowing, when the trauma buffer saturates and breaches, the system demands a reckoning.

Many survivors fear this stage most – because it feels like unraveling. In truth, it's the necessary undoing of false scaffolding so that something real can be built in its place.

Stage 3: Conscious Reconstruction

Here, the survivor, often for the first time, consciously questions:

- What adaptations served me, and what are they costing me now?
- What is mine, and what was imposed upon me by trauma, culture, or family systems?
- What parts of me need grieving before they can be integrated?

This stage is tough because it demands agency. No longer can blame or bitterness alone sustain movement. The survivor begins to take ownership of the healing journey that trauma never asked permission to set into motion.

New practices of gaining agency begin with:

- Breathwork to regulate a hyper-reactive nervous system.
- Physical movement to reclaim body autonomy and rebuild confidence.
- Nutrition to repair what survival mode degraded.
- Authentic connection to replace isolation with resonance.

These practices are always immediately fruitful. But over time, they create small nodes of stability, scaffolding a new internal reality that is less reactive and more responsive.

Stage 4: Expansion of Privilege Plasticity

Privilege plasticity, the ability to dream, risk, and adapt toward expansion rather than survival, begins to take root.

This stage includes:

- Developing tolerance for uncertainty without immediate threat perception.
- Practicing self-trust after a lifetime of conditional trust relationships.
- Consciously identifying triggers, negative self-talk, catastrophizing, and self-sabotage.
- Redefining success metrics to include rest, pleasure, creativity, and relational depth.
- Building relationships based on mutuality rather than utility.

The survivor no longer acts primarily out of fear of loss, shame, or avoiding annihilation. They act, imperfectly but intentionally, out of vision, values, and self-anchored purpose.

The privilege of plasticity is not the absence of trauma memory. It's the development of enough internal and external resources that the past no longer dictates every decision, every mood, every breath.

Stage 5: Self-Reclamation

At this final, and lifelong, stage, the survivor-turned-thriver understands that healing is about becoming someone evolved – returning to the person they were meant to be before survival carved its demands into their nervous system and integrating it with the scarred dreamer seen in the mirror.

Reclamation looks like:

- Grieving the lost timelines without drowning in them.
- Celebrating the small, often invisible victories.
- Refusing to measure progress by capitalist productivity standards.
- Restoring ancestral wisdom about community, rhythm, and resilience.
- Holding boundaries without apology.
- Nurturing a future where lineage will carry less survival plasticity, and more of the generative freedom privilege plasticity offers.

Sacred reclamation is less flashy than the "transformation" narratives so often sold to trauma survivors. It's quieter. Humbler. Deeper.

It's about becoming rooted in the self, the body, the present, the possibilities.

The arc is not a ladder. It's a spiral. We revisit each stage throughout life. We regress when systems fail us anew. We expand when conditions allow. We master not through erasure of trauma but through a continuous, living relationship with it.

Healing is not perfection. Healing is presence.

The journey from the edge winds forever. But it leads toward sacred ground. And you, dear reader, have already taken the first steps.

The Practical Blueprint

Small Daily Revolutions

THIS BOOK WAS NEVER intended to remain theoretical. Theories, no matter how elegant, mean nothing if they cannot be embodied.

Healing from survival-driven plasticity requires action. Not random action. Not frenzied self-help chasing. **Precise, layered, grounded action** – built on a deep understanding of how trauma reshapes physiology, cognition, and relational dynamics.

The Blueprint is simple, but not easy. It's broken into four foundational pillars: **Breath, Movement, Nutrition, and Connection.**

These are not wellness buzzwords. They are the physical languages of survival and healing. They are the means by which the nervous system can be repatterned, the body re-inhabited, and the soul brought back from the periphery to the center.

Each pillar will be explained not only for its practical application but also for its neurobiological and sociological significance. Trauma rewires the system for fear and contraction. The Blueprint is a map back to expansion and conscious living.

Pillar One: *Breath* – Reclaiming Autonomic Sovereignty

Trauma survivors often live in a body that is preparing for war even when no battle is imminent. Breath becomes shallow, rapid, thoracic. The diaphragm, the muscle most responsible for deep, restorative breathing, tightens. Over time, the body forgets how to signal safety to itself.

Breath is not optional for healing. It's the gateway.

Slow, deep, diaphragmatic breathing is one of the few conscious actions that can directly influence the autonomic nervous system, the system responsible for fight, flight, freeze, and faint responses.

Reclaiming breath does several things:

- Lowers sympathetic (fight/flight) dominance.
- Increases parasympathetic (rest/digest) activation.
- Improves heart rate variability (HRV), a biomarker of resilience.
- Restores the body's ability to shift states flexibly – the biological hallmark of privilege plasticity.

Practical Application:

- **Box Breathing** (4 seconds inhale, 4 hold, 4 exhale, 4 hold) – 2-5 minutes, twice daily.
- **Extended Exhales** (inhale 4, exhale 6) to trigger vagal tone and soothe the system.
- **Sighing Protocols** – a simple double inhale through the nose followed by a slow exhale through the mouth, to reset stress responses in real time.

Breath becomes a ritual of remembrance. I am alive. I am here. I am no longer trapped in the battlefield of my origins.

Pillar Two: *Movement* – Rebuilding Trust with the Body

Trauma severs the relationship between the mind and body. Many survivors dissociate, freeze, or ignore bodily signals until they escalate into dysfunction.

Movement, when approached with intention and compassion, reestablishes this relationship.

Movement is not about performance. It's about **presence**.

Why Movement Matters:

- Physical activity releases brain-derived neurotrophic factor (BDNF), a protein that supports neuroplasticity.
- Joint and tissue movement increases proprioceptive signaling, grounding the survivor in time and space.
- Movement allows for discharge of pent-up sympathetic arousal that otherwise stagnates into anxiety, depression, or chronic pain.

Practical Application:

- **Micro-movement**: 60-second stretches or mobility drills during work breaks.
- **Joyful movement**: dance, martial arts, walking in nature – movements that restore pleasure and autonomy.
- **Trauma-sensitive exercise**: activities like tai chi, yoga, or qigong that combine breath, flow, and awareness.

Every step, every reach, every conscious shift in posture says: This body is mine. This life is mine.

Pillar Three: *Nutrition* – Repairing the Internal Landscape

Survival mode depletes essential resources. Chronic stress impairs digestion, gut health, nutrient absorption, and hormonal regulation.

Nutrition is not just about calories or weight. It's about **cellular repair and signal optimization.**

A dysregulated gut-brain axis, common in trauma survivors, perpetuates inflammation, mood instability, and energy crashes. Rebuilding the internal terrain is necessary to support sustained healing.

Key Nutritional Focus Areas:

- **Blood sugar regulation:** high-protein, fiber-rich meals to stabilize energy and mood.
- **Anti-inflammatory eating:** prioritizing colorful vegetables, omega-3 fatty acids, and minimizing ultra-processed foods.
- **Gut support:** probiotics from fermented foods (if tolerated), bone broth, collagen, and prebiotic fibers.

Practical Application:

- Start the day with 20-30g of protein within an hour of waking.
- Hydrate strategically – not just water, but mineral-rich fluids to replenish adrenal resilience.
- Reduce refined sugars and caffeine during active healing phases to lower nervous system reactivity.

Every bite becomes an act of rebellion against the forces that once taught the body it was expendable.

Pillar Four: *Connection* – Restoring Safe Belonging

One of the most devastating impacts of trauma is relational injury. The rupture of safe attachment, the shattering of trust.

Healing can't occur in isolation. It's a relational phenomenon.

Why Connection is Non-Negotiable:

- Co-regulation is the process by which nervous systems synchronize and is a primary means of emotional and physiological regulation.
- Community provides buffering against existential despair and systemic injustice.
- Authentic connection counteracts the loneliness and alienation that weaponized survival often instills.

The global pandemic of COVID-19 further amplified what was already a simmering epidemic of loneliness, disconnection, and relational fragmentation. Social distancing measures, while necessary to limit viral spread, severed millions from their sources of co-regulation and collective grounding. Virtual connection – though a partial salve – could not fully substitute for the embodied, nuanced, multi-sensory reality of human presence. Many survivors, already skilled at masking their internal struggles, found themselves adrift without the casual rituals of interaction that had once masked the depth of their isolation.

Post-pandemic, the landscape of connection remains altered. Trust in institutions, in communities, and even sometimes in each other has eroded. Many survivors find themselves hesitant to rebuild. This hesitancy is understandable, but remaining isolated is a slow form of spiritual and physiological decay.

Practical Application:

- **Layered vulnerability:** sharing selectively with trusted individuals rather than impulsively oversharing or chronically hiding.
- **Ritualized community:** regularly scheduled gatherings – even casual ones – to re-anchor the self in collective humanity.
- **Boundaried generosity:** helping and serving others without self-erasure, maintaining emotional currency reserves.
- **Physical presence when possible:** prioritizing in-person connection over virtual where safely possible, honoring the necessity of human touch, eye contact, and shared energetic fields for full nervous system restoration.

Every connection stitched back into the fabric of life repairs a small part of the original wound. Every courageous step toward community is an act of sacred defiance against the forces that seek to keep us divided, isolated, and diminished.

The Blueprint Is Not Linear

There is no fixed order. Some days breath will be the only practice accessible. Some seasons will demand more movement, others deeper connection.

The point is not perfection.

The point is presence.

Healing is not a self-improvement project. It's the restoration of the original birthright: to exist without apology, to belong without bartering, to breathe without bracing.

FINAL BLESSING

If you made it here, I am proud of you. Proud the way a man is proud of someone who took every punch life could throw and still got back up. Proud because you did not let the weight break you. You are standing. Maybe bruised, maybe tired, but standing.

Healing is not pretty work. It's not made for public applause. It happens in quiet spaces when no one is looking. It asks for things the world rarely rewards: patience, humility, forgiveness. It asks you to sit with your pain long enough to understand it instead of running from it.

There will be days when all you can do is breathe and get through. There will be days when you wonder if it's even worth it. Those days count. Every day you show up to your own becoming counts.

You are not too late. You are not too broken. You are not defined by what hurt you.

Keep walking. Keep choosing yourself even when it feels easier to quit. Keep believing there is more to your story than survival.

May your nights be lighter and your mornings less heavy. May you feel your own goodness rising in your chest like a song you forgot you knew. May you find the courage to build a life from love, not fear. May you become, with all your scars and dreams, the living proof that healing is possible.

And when you are ready, reach back. Somebody else needs your light to find their way.

Epilogue

The Journey Ahead

HEALING IS NOT A finite project. It's not a finish line you cross triumphantly, arms raised, free forevermore from the scars and echoes of your past. Healing is a long journey that twists back upon itself, one that demands detours, rest stops, and periods of necessary retreat. It's the road back to yourself, paved with choices to reclaim what was stolen, lost, or surrendered along the way.

For those who have lived through weaponized survival, the task is personal recovery and reconstruction. It's the painstaking, sacred work of building new pathways in a nervous system trained to expect betrayal, violence, scarcity, and shame. It's learning to trust safety when it finally appears, to recognize opportunity when your trauma-trained mind insists it's danger, and to move toward community when the old reflex tells you to isolate.

The journey of a trauma survivor is a story of loss. And it's a story of profound wisdom – resilience honed under conditions that would have broken most. The story of how adaptive strategies – the masks, the costumes, the compulsions – were never failures, but ingenious attempts to survive in an environment not built for your thriving. And a story of how survival plasticity was an overachievement in the face of systemic neglect and harm.

The journey from the edge is an active reclamation. A reaching back to the child you were before the fractures and betrayals. A gathering of the parts you buried because you had no choice. It's about becoming the parent, the protector, the champion for your inner child that no one else could be. It's about taking the scars and using them not to harm others, but to carve a new map leading others out of their own closets of pain and into sacred, sovereign reclamation.

This journey is long because the forces that weaponized survival are still alive. Systemic injustice, economic disparities, social betrayals, political regression did not end with your personal awakening. They still push against the fragile soil you are trying to till and make fertile again. This is why community is not optional. This is why solidarity among survivors, Rooted Reclaimers, is not merely a feel-good concept, but a necessity.

The journey is not fair. It's not linear. It will not reward you for your suffering automatically. But if you commit to it, if you breathe when you want to run, if you move when you want to freeze, if you nourish yourself when your reflex is self-deprivation, if you connect when your instinct is to withdraw, then you will reclaim something sacred. You will reclaim your own life.

You will not be who you were before the fracture. That innocence is gone, and mourning it is holy work. But you will become something else – someone rooted, resilient, expansive. You will not just survive. You will write yourself back into the story of your own life, as neither victim nor hero, but as a sovereign human being who has faced down annihilation and chosen life anyway.

The journey ahead will ask everything of you. And it will give you back everything that matters.

Not all at once. Not without cost. But enough. Enough to live not in reaction, but in creation.

Enough to reclaim your life, and to build a life worthy of the sacred soul you have fought to protect across impossible distances.

Thank you for taking this journey with me.

ROOTED RECLAIMERS

Thank You

FOR WALKING THIS PATH

If you've made it to the end of this book,
I'd love to hear from you:

Would you consider
leaving a short review on Amazon?

Reviews help this work reach those who most need it, especially those who feel isolated in their survival patterns.

You can leave a review here:

RootedReclaimers.com/Review

— *(or simply search the book and click "Write a Review")*

A few honest sentences is all it takes

Thank you for helping others
find their way back to themselves.

Acknowledgments

To my wife, my love, thank you for your unwavering belief in me and enduring with me.
To my little prince, William Pierce, your light and laughter have been a constant anchor.
To my father, my brother, and my sister, who have helped me in immeasurable ways.
To Dr. Michele Renée, my business partner, thank you for holding the vision when the way forward was uncertain.
To my fraternity, Alpha Phi Alpha Fraternity, Inc., thank you for shaping the legacy that made this work possible.
To every colleague, friend, mentor, elder, and patient who encouraged me along the way – your belief in my voice gave me the strength to get these thoughts onto paper.
And to every Rooted Reclaimer – those who are quietly breaking generational cycles, choosing restoration over performance, and daring to build sacred ground in a world still healing from its own wounds – this book is yours.

Glossary

Adaptations as Strengths

Survival behaviors initially formed for protection, later mistaken for inherent character strengths when they are actually responses to trauma.

> Sometimes the things we pride ourselves on – our stoicism, our perfectionism, our humor – are really just clever survival strategies we developed to stay safe.

Connoisseur of Injustice

A person who has developed acute sensitivity to patterns of unfairness and systemic threat due to lived experience navigating oppressive systems.

> Being a connoisseur of injustice means you can read a room, a face, a policy – and immediately sense the hidden dangers others might miss.

Emotional Currency

The internal psychological and emotional resources expended to maintain a façade of normalcy, safety, or success in hostile or oppressive environments.

> Emotional currency is the invisible cost we pay to survive and appear "normal" – the energy spent hiding our fear, regulating others' comfort, and performing resilience.

Existential Unfairness

A profound realization that systemic injustice is not accidental or occasional but embedded into the very structure of societal life.

> Existential unfairness is the gut-punch moment when you realize the world isn't just occasionally unfair – it was built unfairly from the ground up.

Invisible Fractures

The unseen psychological and emotional wounds left by prolonged survival experiences, often masked by external success.

> Invisible fractures are the cracks you can't see – the parts of yourself you had to abandon just to keep moving forward, even when it looked like you were thriving.

Neural Cost of Survival

The cognitive and neurological toll exacted by prolonged hypervigilance and survival mode living, resulting in reduced adaptability and emotional availability.

> The neural cost of survival is the brain fog, fatigue, and emotional flatness that happen when you've been running on fear for too long.

Primary Coping Mechanism

The dominant behavioral or emotional strategy an individual unconsciously adopts to survive repeated or ongoing trauma.

> Your primary coping mechanism is the go-to behavior you built to survive hard things – whether that's shutting down, lashing out, overachieving, or disappearing inside yourself.

Privilege Plasticity

An advantageous pattern of neuroplastic development enabled by safe environments, allowing risk-taking, innovation, and long-term growth without the burden of constant threat vigilance.

> Privilege plasticity is the gift of growing up without constant danger – when your brain and body are free to risk, dream, and explore, instead of staying locked in survival mode.

Survival Plasticity

A pattern of neural and behavioral adaptation focused on threat detection and immediate survival, limiting cognitive and emotional growth capacities.

> Survival plasticity means your brain adapts to survive threats first and foremost, leaving little space for creativity, dreaming, or expansion. It's survival mode hardwired into your nervous system.

Survival Story

The narrative constructed around one's ability to endure hardship, often glorified externally but internally masking unhealed trauma.

> A survival story is what we tell the world – and sometimes ourselves – about how strong we are, while hiding how much it cost us to stay alive.

The Closet

A somatic space within the body where unprocessed trauma isolates itself, contributing to physiological dysfunction through inflammation and immune dysregulation.

> "The Closet" is the hidden place in the body where trauma gets trapped – in organs, fascia, joints, and tissues – festering beneath the surface and triggering physical and emotional reactions.

The Emotional Buffer

An internal psychological barrier that absorbs chronic micro and macro aggressions, injustices, and traumas, protecting conscious awareness until overwhelmed.

> The emotional buffer is like a shock absorber for life's unfairness – it protects you from feeling the full weight of every injustice until it slowly wears thin.

The Journey from the Edge

The slow, non-linear journey of healing, reclaiming authenticity, and reconnecting to one's original self after trauma.

> The journey from the edge isn't a straight path – it's the messy, sacred journey of finding your way back to who you were before the world taught you to hide.

Trauma Architecture

The systemic, structural design by which trauma is culturally transmitted, reinforced, and normalized across generations.

> Trauma architecture is the way our world is built – not by accident, but by design – to pass down pain and survival adaptations generation after generation.

Trauma Buffer

A dynamic psychological threshold where cumulative traumatic stress is absorbed until the system (mind/body) can no longer contain it.

> The trauma buffer is like a dam inside you, holding back the floodwaters of everything you've endured – until one day, it cracks under the weight.

Trauma Economics

The disproportionate emotional, cognitive, and financial burden placed on individuals and communities repeatedly exposed to systemic injustice.

> Trauma economics is the extra toll people from marginalized groups pay – in energy, in opportunity, even in years of their lives – just trying to stay afloat.

Research and Reflections

- Smith, Will and Mark Manson. *Will*. Penguin Press, 2021.
- NPR. "Will Smith Opens Up About His Memoir and What He's Learned." Nov 10, 2021. npr.org
- PEOPLE. "Tyler Perry Reflects on Childhood Trauma and Intensive Therapy." March 2024. people.com
- The Academy of Motion Picture Arts and Sciences. "94th Oscars Telecast." March 27, 2022.
- Paley Center for Media. "Tyler Perry Honored: A Conversation on Art, Impact, and Healing." 2024.
- U.S. News & World Report. "How Childhood Trauma Affects Adult Mental Health." 2022.
- Harvard Health. "The Long-Term Effects of Childhood Trauma." 2021.
- Perry, Tyler. Various interviews and speeches, 2020–2024.
- van der Kolk, Bessel. *The Body Keeps the Score: Brain, Mind, and Body in the Healing of Trauma*. Penguin Books, 2014.
- Porges, Stephen. *The Polyvagal Theory: Neurophysiological Foundations of Emotions, Attachment, Communication, Self-Regulation*. Norton, 2011.

- Levine, Peter A. *Waking the Tiger: Healing Trauma*. North Atlantic Books, 1997.
- Mehling, W. E., et al. "Body Awareness: A Phenomenological Inquiry into the Common Ground of Mind-Body Therapies." *Philosophy, Ethics, and Humanities in Medicine*, vol. 6, 2011.

ROOTED RECLAIMERS

KEEP GOING — WITH COMMUNITY

You don't have to heal alone.

If you'd like to continue this journey with gentle support and a community that understands, join us inside the Rooted Reclaimers Commons:

- Monthly live practice sessions
- Access to the Four Pillars workbooks
- Clinician-informed tools
- A trauma-informed, moderated space
- Optional AI companions for reflection and rehearsal

Learn more & join us at:

RootedReclaimers.com/Community

— Small moves. Sacred ground. —

Body-first. Equity-centered. Community-held.

Breathe Move Nourish Connect

Rooted Reclaimers ►

Made in the USA
Monee, IL
13 September 2026

62981879R10095